DIALOGUE WITH
NORTH KOREA?

ASIA INSIGHTS

A series aimed at increasing an understanding of contemporary Asia among policy-makers, NGOs, businesses, journalists and other members of the general public as well as scholars and students.

1. *Ideas, Society and Politics in Northeast Asia and Northern Europe: Worlds Apart, Learning From Each Other*, edited by Ras Tind Nielsen and Geir Helgesen

2. *The Shanghai Cooperation Organization and Eurasian Geopolitics: New Directions, Perspectives, and Challenges*, edited by Michael Fredholm

3. *Burma/Myanmar – Where Now?*, edited by Mikael Gravers and Flemming Ytzen

4. *Dialogue with North Korea? Preconditions for Talking Human Rights With a Hermit Kingdom*, by Geir Helgesen and Hatla Thelle

5. *After the Great East Japan Earthquake: Political and Policy Change in Post-Fukushima Japan*, edited by Dominic Al-Badri and Gijs Berends

NIAS Press is the autonomous publishing arm of NIAS – Nordic Institute of Asian Studies, a research institute located at the University of Copenhagen. NIAS is partially funded by the governments of Denmark, Finland, Iceland, Norway and Sweden via the Nordic Council of Ministers, and works to encourage and support Asian studies in the Nordic countries. In so doing, NIAS has been publishing books since 1969, with more than two hundred titles produced in the past few years.

UNIVERSITY OF COPENHAGEN

Nordic Council of Ministers

DIALOGUE WITH NORTH KOREA?

Preconditions for Talking Human Rights With a Hermit Kingdom

Geir Helgesen and Hatla Thelle

Nordic Institute of Asian Studies
Asia Insights series, no. 4

First published in 2013 by NIAS Press
NIAS – Nordic Institute of Asian Studies
Øster Farimagsgade 5, 1353 Copenhagen K, Denmark
Tel: +45 3532 9501 • Fax: +45 3532 9549
E-mail: books@nias.ku.dk • Online: www.niaspress.dk

A CIP catalogue record for this book is available from the British Library

ISBN: 978-87-7694-126-0 (pbk)

Typeset in Arno Pro 12/15.6 and Frutiger 11/13.2
Typesetting by NIAS Press
Printed in the United Kingdom by Marston Digital

*Cover illustration: A small gathering on the edge of Pyongyang
(photo: Geir Helgesen)*

Contents

Table

Illustrations

The photograph of Kim Jong Il and Madeleine Albright (p. 25) © Reuters. All other photographs © Geir Helgesen.

Acknowledgements

We are grateful to the people we met in North Korea, working in different government agencies, for giving *their* views on matters of common interests, for putting up with difficult inquiries, and for their willingness, after all, to discuss issues that in their country are perceived to be highly controversial. We are obviously indebted to colleagues around the world with whom we have discussed matters related to what we present in this book, none mentioned, none forgotten.

Some names have to be mentioned, and among them political scientist Ras Tind Nielsen, who has done a great job in editing the first version of the manuscript; thanks to him we realized that this book fills a void in the debates on North Korea and the world. Thanks, too, to Liz Bramsen for her language editing. Gianluca Spezza from the University of Torino, now at Turku University, Finland, read the manuscript and came up with some important suggestions that have improved the end result. Furthermore, together with NIAS Press, he produced an exciting map of North Korean ´burning issues´. Our Editor in Chief, Gerald Jackson, has put a lot of effort and creativity, as he always does, to make this product good looking and readable. We, the authors, are solely responsible for the content, and any errors are our own.

We are most grateful for warm support and good advice from the Danish Institute for Human Rights along the way, as well as for ideas, input and suggestions from colleagues at NIAS – the Nordic Institute of Asian Studies. Last but certainly not least, we thank the Korea Foundation for supporting this project, despite its uncertain outcome.

As outsiders it is our sincere hope that with this publication we might contribute to a broader understanding of a complicated conflict and introduce some novel perspectives and ideas. The book is dedicated to all actors in Korea and outside the peninsula who believe in and work for enhanced understanding between the parties concerned and who maintain that positive solutions are possible, if trust and human creativity are invested.

Prologue

There is hardly another country as isolated and with such a bleak image as North Korea. It is portrayed in the Western media as a hermit kingdom[1] ruled by an outdated communist dictatorship whose clandestine nuclear programmes alarm its neighbours and whose dreadful labour camps keep control of a population wracked by famine. The regime's poor track record on human rights is stressed time and again by both Western governments and international organizations. Prospects look bleak for any improvement in relations, let alone the initiation of a dialogue on human rights.

Offering a more nuanced analysis of the North Korean situation, this study argues that not only is a constructive and fruitful dialogue on human rights possible but it is also desir-

1. A hermit is a person who lives in seclusion from society, and accordingly the term 'hermit kingdom' applies to a country that willfully seeks isolation from the rest of the world. The traditional Korea was frequently in the West described as a hermit kingdom during the latter part of the Yi dynasty (1392–1910). The term may still be used by Koreans themselves to describe pre-modern Korea but it is also used by outsiders to describe North Korea today. For example, in her memoir *Madam Secretary*, former US Secretary of State Madeleine Albright entitles the chapter on her visit to North Korea 'Inside the Hermit Kingdom'. When we use the term in the title of this publication, it is because it has now become a catchphrase for North Korea in Western news media, and by using it we want to emphasize that we see the continued isolation as disadvantageous for a positive development in the country and in the region.

able for both parties. New perspectives are provided on the general perception of North Korea, its relationship to the international human rights regime, the rationales that underpin decision-making in international relations, and the perceptions and expectations of people occupying official positions in the North Korean bureaucracy. The authors also draw from previous experiences to suggest ways in which a dialogue could be established and to point out specific areas where it would be realistic. They point to valuable lessons to be learned from the dialogue so far between North Korea and the UN system of human rights as well as from experiences gained in the already established EU–China human rights dialogue.

Key findings

North Korea's behaviour in international relations is greatly affected by the actions and reactions of the outside world. This also goes for its compliance/non-compliance with the human rights regime. A stronger North Korean commitment to the UN human rights system has occurred when key international players – the US, South Korea and the EU – have chosen a conciliatory approach towards the North over an antagonistic one.

Contrary to what is generally maintained in the media, our experience is that North Korean diplomats, officials and professionals welcome outside help and reflect a considerable willingness to cooperate with international partners. However, there is also widespread agreement among foreign actors with working experience from North Korea that it takes time to develop positive relations with the people of that country. Only when such positive relations are established will it be possible to reach positive practical results.

When discussing human rights issues with North Korea, Western governments need to adopt a pragmatic approach that separates sensitive and non-sensitive issues and deal with them accordingly. While insistence on a free media or political rights would probably lead to a total breakdown of communication before it even began, working to set up frameworks for low-key and concrete cooperation projects in areas related to food production, public health or energy could greatly improve living conditions for the North Korean population.

Due to the existing animosities and conflicting relations that currently characterize contacts between North Korea and the outside world, we deem improvement of conditions for the North Korean people to be the common responsibility of the authorities in Pyongyang and governments in our part of the world. Taking the urgent needs of the North Korea population as the point of departure, and based on previous experiences with North Korea's foreign relations, we argue that a positive Western initiative to end the stalemate would be the best way of aiding the people living in North Korea, as well as an important step towards creating a base for the normalization of relations between North Korea and the world.

© NIAS Press 2013

Issues and opportunities in the Korean peninsula

❶   Rason Special Economic Zone, established 1991 based on cities of
    Rajin and Sonbong. Results have fallen behind expectations but pros-
    pects are good. The SEZ is one of the few ice-free ports in the area
    (the others being Chongjin and Vladivostok) and its proximity to the
    Yanbian K.A.P. ❸ makes it a potential hub for the future development
    of North Korea and NE China. Its business school trains selected
    North Koreans in international trade and business practices.

❷   Chongjin, the capital of North Hamgyong Province and the country's
    third largest city. Sometimes called the 'City of Iron' due to its past as a
    centre for steel and other heavy industry. Apart from Rason ❶ the only
    other ice-free port in the northern area.

❸   China's Yanbian Korean Autonomous Prefecture (capital Yanji), desig-
    nated thus due to the large number of ethnic Koreans living there. An
    established centre of unofficial and semi-official border trade, esp. in
    areas where the Tumen river is easy to cross.

❹ Sinŭiju, capital of North Pyeongan Province, neighbours Dandong in China. Part of the city is included in a Special Administrative Region established in 2002 to experiment with introducing a market economy.

❺ The Yongbyon Nuclear Scientific Research Centre is North Korea's major nuclear facility, operating its first nuclear reactors. It produced the fissile material for nuclear weapon tests in 2006 and 2009, and since 2009 has developed indigenous light-water nuclear power technology.

❻ Location of the sinking of the R.O.K. warship *Cheonan* on 26 March 2010 near Baengnyeong Island in the Yellow Sea, killing 46 seamen.

❼ Kaesong Industrial Park, a special administrative industrial region established in 2002. The economic cooperation project is an example of inter-Korean cooperation that has managed to survive despite relations between the two sides hitting an all-time low after the sinking of the *Cheonan* ❼ and shelling of Yeonpyeong Island ❽.

⑧ Yeonpyeong Island, located near the **NLL** and only 12 km from the North Korean coastline. On 23 November 2010, North Korean artillery shelled Yeonpyeong in response to a R.O.K. military exercise in the area. Two R.O.K. marines and two civilians were killed. The episode is the closest the two sides have got to war since the 1953 armistice.

❾ Dokdo (*Jap:* Takeshima), whose Korean sovereignty is disputed by Japan. Many Koreans also claim Tsushima Island (*Kor:* Daemado) to be Korean but no legal dispute currently exists between the countries.

DMZ   The Demilitarized Zone, running across the Korean Peninsula roughly at the 38th Parallel, serves as a buffer zone between North and South Korea. Created as part of the 1953 armistice, the DMZ is probably the most militarized area in the world today.

NLL   The Northern Limit Line is a disputed (but de facto) maritime demarcation line in the Yellow Sea between North and South Korea.

❖ North Korean detention camps (*Kwanliso*). North Korea denies the existence of such camps or indeed of any penal labour colonies. According to other sources, the *Kwanliso* is one of three forms of political imprisonment in the country, there being an 150,000 to 200,000 political prisoners in total. The condemned are said to be sent to *Kwanliso* without any form of judicial process. The most common form of punishment for those sent to the camps seems to be forced labour. Duties within *Kwanliso* typically include work in mines (e.g. coal, gold and iron ore), forestry or agriculture.

▲ Baekdusan (or Mount Baekdu), the highest peak on the Korean peninsula. This straddles the Sino-Korean border. Koreans on both sides of the peninsula consider it a holy place. North Korea's official historiography claims that Kim Jong Il was born in a secret military camp on the slopes of the mountain while Soviet records and other sources indicate that he was born in Russia near Khabarovsk.

Annotation of map and associated notes prepared by Gianluca Spezza

Preconditions for a Constructive Dialogue

*H*ow to establish conditions for a constructive dialogue with North Korea on human rights? Are human rights something that North Korean government officials even care about? If so, what are the main obstacles to a dialogue on the issue? These are some of the questions that this book tries to answer. The aim is to provide different perspectives on the general perception of North Korea, its relationship to the international human rights regime and the bureaucrats populating its political system, and then to draw on concrete experiences to suggest ways in which a dialogue could be established and in what specific areas it would be realistic. The book is motivated by a visit made to North Korea in October 2010 by Hatla Thelle, Senior Researcher at the Danish Institute for Human Rights and Geir Helgesen, Director of NIAS, the Nordic Institute of Asian Studies, in Copenhagen.

Is Dialogue with North Korea at All Possible?

A constructive dialogue with North Korea on human rights – a dialogue with what is predominantly seen as an irresponsible, unpredictable and aggressive regime unable to create livable conditions for its own population and forcing insecurity and fear on neighbouring people (in short, an evil entity) – seems a mission impossible. However, we do not fully buy the above assumptions, or at least we believe that they are only part of the entire puzzle. Important pieces are missing. An important piece is what could be termed cross-cultural empathy. In an insightful study published under the title 'think no evil' the American social scientist Fred Alford writes:

> An evil other is a welcome idea in the West, giving our dread a face and a place. But such an idea is not welcome in Korea. To call North Korea evil would be impossibly terrifying for most Koreans, because Koreans cannot create the type of distance from the North that would allow them to alienate evil there. North Korea is quite literally still family.[1]

A constructive dialogue with North Korea requires a better understanding of the country and the rationales that underpin its decision-making in international relations.[2] Also required is a better understanding of the people that occupy official positions in the North Korean bureaucracy, their perceptions and expectations. Moreover, there are valuable lessons to be learned from the dialogue so far between North Korea and the UN human rights regime as well as from the experiences of the already established EU–China human rights dialogue.

---

1. C. Fred Alford (1999) *Think No Evil: Korean Values in the Age of Globalization*, Ithaca and London: Cornell University Press, pp.104–105

2. The newly elected South Korean President, Ms Park Geun-hye, who visited Pyongyang and the then North Korean leader Kim Jong Il in 2002, has revealed a belief in dialogue and negotiations without preconditions rather than continued external pressure towards the North with resulting inter-Korean animosities and risks of new conflicts (personal exchange, Copenhagen 2010, Seoul 2011).

The Nordic countries might be in a favourable position to play a positive role vis-à-vis North Korea as we have long-standing diplomatic relations with them and generally enjoy a positive image among North Korean government officials.

Subtle Variations in a One-Sided Picture

This book has not been drafted to endorse the North Korean system, its leadership or their actions. Our aim is to challenge the existing one-sided pictures and to pinpoint the subtle variations in an apparent monolithic reality. This is because we see these very pictures – the one promoted by North Korean propaganda and the opposite one promoted by Western media – as both too one-sided and unrealistically positive or negative to reasonably depict the given reality, and thus as major hindrances to establishing a constructive dialogue. Our main reason for publishing the following pages is concern for the living conditions for the approximately 23 million people living between the 38th parallel and the Chinese border, a number equivalent to the population of all five Nordic countries put together. The political system in Pyongyang is considered an enemy of the free world, but does that mean that the people of North Korea are also our enemies? The western world in effect treats them as if they were, by not utilizing every possible opening to positively influence the situation This is a mistake. The Nordic countries have an obligation with regard to North Korea and its population, as we established diplomatic relations with Pyongyang back in the mid-1970s. The idea at that time must have been that regardless of the character of the system, isolation is negative and dialogue is positive.

Our ambition here, then, is to identify the preconditions necessary to such a dialogue. We bring to the table the experience of two senior researchers: Hatla Thelle, historian and China scholar who has worked for years with Chinese and European colleagues to create a human rights dialogue with China, and who, when a dialogue was established, has taken part in it on various levels; and Geir Helgesen, cultural sociologist and long-term Korea observer who has travelled extensively in both Koreas, organized Track II dialogues between North Korea and the Nordic countries, and maintained a global network of colleagues who deal with the divided Korea. While Hatla has experienced relative success in her work on human rights in China, Geir can only argue that the North Koreans would welcome a similar dialogue on the basis of his contacts with their country over the years.

We visited North Korea in late 2010 to identify hindrances and discuss possibilities for cooperation and dialogue. We held talks with government officials from various ministries. Many items were touched upon, some introduced by us, others by the North Koreans. Some were controversial, for example, questions regarding the human rights situation in particular. Others were straightforward and related to issues as diverse as health, agriculture, trade, environmental protection and cooperation with international organizations. Obviously, the North Korean officials we met represented the regime, but they did not necessarily echo the preferences of the then supreme leader only. While North Korea is unfamiliar and difficult to comprehend for Western observers, the image of a totalitarian and monolithic country lacking any kind of human touch is not only wrong but also dangerous.

North Koreans are human beings, too. Their socio-cultural environment is different from ours, different from the socio-cultural environment in most countries. This is due to both internal and external conditions, some politically decided, others the consequence of historical forces and the result of international conflicts. To some extent North Korea remains a hostage of the Cold War and a victim of the consequences of the Korean War. The North Koreans occupy half of the peninsula's territory and have to compete with a stronger, richer and more developed other half for the legitimacy of their regime. It would be conducive to dialogue and peace if all parties took this contemporary situation as the point of departure.

A Role for the Nordic Countries to Play

Coming from the opposite side of the Eurasian continent, one might ask how we (Europe and in particular the Nordic countries) can contribute to aiding and assisting North Korea and the Korean peninsula on the whole in easing tension and improving the situation of its people? As we see it, there are three main reasons why we should be concerned and investigate ways of supporting improved relations and establishing a human rights dialogue between North Korea and the outside world:

- The North Korean population is in great need of humanitarian assistance and as global citizens we are obliged to help people in need.
- The Nordic countries have had diplomatic relations with North Korea since the mid-1970s, longer than most states in the Western world. This obliges us to pay particular attention to the situation there.
- The Nordic welfare states are in a position to inspire North Korea in its ongoing search for a sustainable reform agenda.

Here it is important to emphasize Nordic regionalism, where competing countries with a history of war and conflict have developed a strong, popularly endorsed regional system of cooperation that might not only inspire North Korea in its relationship with its neighbours but also create a basis for mutual relations between the other nations of Northeast Asia.

The Structure of the Book

In this book we argue that a constructive dialogue on human rights with North Korea is possible. For this to take place, however, one should take the following points into consideration. In the first chapter, we emphasize the need to improve and contextualize the understanding of North Korea's behaviour in international politics before Western governments engage in dialogue with North Korea on the human rights issue. We argue that to a large extent North Korea's experiences with the outside world affect its behaviour regarding dialogues with outside powers. For example, the initiation of the South Korean Sunshine Policy and the relatively open approach of the Clinton administration resulted in a more open North Korean attitude towards the international community. Yet, more recent negative experiences, such as Bush's labelling North Korea part of the 'Axis of Evil' combined with a more hardline US approach to the unresolved nuclear issue greatly affected the regime in the opposite direction. In this sense, North Korea's behaviour could be characterized as 'tit-for-tat'; positive actions beget positive reactions and negative actions beget negative reactions. This has implications for the practicability of a human rights dialogue since a minimum level of trust and openness between parties is required. Moreover, we stress that a social science perspective can contribute to our understanding of North Korean actions and reactions and provide some much needed cultural interpretations of North Korean attitudes towards human rights.

In the second chapter, we analyse the interaction between North Korea and the UN human rights regime and address some of the difficulties and hindrances to a fruitful dialogue that are found on both sides of the table. We find that efforts to invite cooperation are difficult, if not impossible, when one party (in this case, North Korea) is one-sidedly singled out as a gross violator through the adoption of UN resolutions. Establishing a constructive and sustainable human rights dialogue requires both sides to adopt a careful approach that takes the trade-off between cooperation and confrontation into thorough consideration.

In the third chapter, we draw on experiences from the EU–China human rights dialogues that have taken place since 1998 to make recommendations for setting up similar talks with North Korea. We argue that 'human rights' cannot be treated as an all-or-nothing question when dealing with North Korea (or other autocratic regimes, for that matter). We should instead adopt a pragmatic approach to human rights; differentiating sensitive and non-sensitive issues and dealing with them accordingly. This is necessary so that the parties can set realistic goals and engage in concrete and practical communication.

In the fourth chapter, we draw on experiences from our recent visit to North Korea. We illustrate that attitudes among North Korean bureaucrats are not as monolithic as speculations and claims made by media outlets and intelligence agencies would have us believe. Rather, there are growing and important generational differences between North Korean bureaucrats and thus different voices when it comes to questions of dialogue with and openness to the outside world. Based on our visit to North Korea in October 2010 and subsequent research, we show that it is important that we understand these voices if we are to engage in constructive dialogue with North Korea. Moreover, we identify areas related to the human rights situation in North Korea in which cooperation and dialogue are both greatly needed and even welcomed by the North Koreans. For example, cooperation in areas such as agriculture, public health care and green energy could greatly improve the living conditions of the North Korean population and thus have a direct impact on human rights in the country.

The fifth chapter offers our conclusions and some perspectives for future action based on the findings of this book.

The Need for Realistic Expectations

Obviously, there are limitations to how much the outside world can change North Korea. We do not argue that promoting a constructive dialogue will allow the human rights situation to change radically. Rather, we argue that a constructive dialogue carried out carefully and under the right circumstances is the first step towards gradual positive changes. Such changes, we believe, are possible once the parties involved are invited to take on a pragmatic, rather than dogmatic, approach to the question.

There is obviously no scientifically correct approach to North Korea; involvement stands as the opposite of containment, and the choice between the two is both a moral and a political one. For governments to engage in constructive dialogue with North Korea, however, we argue that it is necessary to understand the country's special circumstances as well as how cultural differences between 'them' and 'us' impact the conditions for communication.

CHAPTER 1

North Korea Contextualized

*N*orth Korea[1] is claimed to be the most isolated country on earth today, and the gap between the way in which the international community sees North Korea and the way in which the North Koreans see themselves is huge. If a constructive dialogue on human rights between the outside world and North Korea is to be created, it is a necessary and urgent task to bridge that gap. Therefore, before entering into a dialogue with North Korea, representatives of Western governments should take a look at the world as it is viewed from Pyongyang. Such an understanding is extremely important in any case, but when it comes to such sensitive issues as human rights, it is even more so. Thus, the purpose of this first chapter is to place North Korea in a relevant historical and cultural context. It provides some insights on how North Korea's past and recent experiences with the outside world to a large extent affect its present behaviour in international relations, and thus also in human rights dialogues. It also aims to contextualize and improve our understanding of North Korea and the rationales of its decision-makers. Here, it is important

---

1.   The official name is the Democratic People's Republic of Korea (DPRK). In the West, the geographical term, North Korea, is commonly used. Since we address a Western readership, we shall henceforth use 'North Korea'.

9

to understand that the individuals who occupy positions throughout the North Korean bureaucracy do not necessarily *only* echo the preferences of the political leadership but that they *also* represent different views on dialogue and involvement with the outside world. After all, systems are populated by people,[2] and people are shaped by their experiences. This goes for North Korean officials as well. Negative experiences promote negative reactions, while positive experiences are usually followed by positive reactions. Using this relational approach to international politics enables us to shift the focus from the actions of one actor to the relations between different actors. We propose that this relational approach is a constructive way of dealing with a world full of differences.

Why is it important to try to see the world as the North Koreans do, when they obviously see things quite differently than we do? The simple answer is that without this effort, communication between them and us[3] may result in grave misunderstandings with possible unfortunate outcomes. An example of how difficult it can be to grasp outcomes based on North Korean political culture from outside the relevant context is discussed in the following section.

International Concern over North Korean Nuclear Power

The two issues that prevent normalization between North Korea and the outside world are its development of nuclear capabilities and its human rights record. The present effort aims

---

2. Lucian Pye (1985) *Asian Power and Politics. The Cultural Dimensions of Authority*. The Belknap Press of Harvard University Press. Cambridge, Mass. and London.

3. By 'us', we denote the Western world writ large, as both Europe and the USA have a similar and insufficient understanding of the North Korean worldview and political culture.

at identifying ways to engage with North Korea on the human rights issue, and we propose a relational approach to this aim. Although we do not intend to discuss the nuclear issue per se, we will touch upon it and the reactions it has triggered, as this example illustrates well the complicated and conflict-ridden relations between North Korea and the US in particular. As will be argued in the following chapters, the two issues are also interlinked in that condemnations of the nuclear programme affect the regime's openness (or lack of same) to discussing human rights.

The following summary is primarily based on the Nuclear Threat Initiative (NTI)[4] report on North Korea and the Chronology of US–North Korea Nuclear and Missile Diplomacy.[5] Already in the 1950s, North Korea started developing its institutional capability for establishing a nuclear programme; for the first 20 years under supervision and technical assistance from the Soviet Union. The two countries signed an agreement in 1959 on the peaceful use of nuclear energy. By the 1970s, however, North Korean engineers were using indigenous technology. In 1977 a safeguard agreement was signed between the International Atomic Energy Agency (IAEA), the Soviet Union and North Korea, and in 1985 Pyongyang signed the Treaty on the Non-Proliferation of Nuclear Weapons (NPT) in exchange for assistance from the Soviet Union in developing light-water nuclear reactors. Again in 1992, an IAEA safeguard was signed by Pyongyang.

According to the 1992 safeguard agreement, North Korea was to deliver a complete list of its nuclear facilities and materials and open these facilities to international inspectors from the IAEA. Neither the list nor the inspections satisfied the IAEA.

4. See www.nti.org/country-profiles/north-Korea/nuclear.
5. See www.armscontrol.org/factsheets/dprkchron.

Pyongyang's answer was to announce its intention to withdraw from the NPT in 1993. This triggered a long-lasting crisis, especially between North Korea and the US. When it was reported that spent fuel rods were removed from the nuclear reactor in Yongbyon, the Clinton administration considered attacking the site from the air to put a stop to the possible military nuclear development in the North. Eight years later, in 2002, then Secretary of Defense William J. Perry and his assistant, defense secretary Ashton B. Carter, revealed in an article in the Washington Post that: 'The two of us, then at Pentagon, readied plans for striking at North Korea's nuclear facilities and for mobilizing hundreds of thousands of American troops for the war that probably would have followed.'[6] Kim Young-sam, the President of South Korea at the time, believes that he may have prevented a war from breaking out. In a radio interview in 2009 he said:

> [A]t the time, the US Navy's 33 destroyers and two aircraft carriers were waiting for an order in the East Sea to bomb the nuclear facilities in Yongbyon. I strongly opposed the military action because I thought it could lead to a full-fledged war on the Korean peninsula. The United States would have gone ahead with the strike without my objection.[7]

The crisis was calmed when former US President Jimmy Carter in June 1994 met with Kim Il Sung in Pyongyang, a meeting that later resulted in the Agreed Framework,[8] in which

---

6. 'Back to the Brink', Perry and Carter in *The Washington Post*, 20 October 2002.

7. *The Korea Times*, 13 April 2009 (www.koreatimes.co.kr/www/news/nation/2009/04/).

8. Delegations of the governments of the US and North Korea held talks in Geneva from 23 September to 21 October 1994, to negotiate an overall resolution of the nuclear issue on the Korean Peninsula. Both sides agreed to attaining the objectives in the 12 August 1994 agreed statement between the US and North Korea and to uphold the principles of the 11 June 1993 joint statement of the US and North Korea

the North agreed to freeze its programmes and allow the IAEA to monitor their actions. They also consented to maintaining a nuclear-free Korean peninsula policy as agreed with the south in 1991 and to remaining a party of the NPT. In return, the US was to lead an international consortium to construct two light-water nuclear power reactors, provide heavy fuel oil to the North until the first reactor was completed (which was scheduled to happen in 2003), and last, but not least, pledge 'formal assurances against the threat or use of nuclear weapons by the US'.[9] While Perry and Carter in the aforementioned article maintain that the Agreed Framework, although controversial and contested, 'ha[s] served our security interests well',[10] it is no secret that both parties (the US and North Korea) were dissatisfied: the US with difficulties in the inspection of the North Korean facilities, North Korea with the slow pace of the construction of the light-water power stations.

Usually, the media report on how North Korea fails to keep its promises, and this makes continued negotiations with the country difficult if not impossible. However, there are also failings on the other side, and Leon V. Sigal, director of the Northeast Asia Cooperative Security Project at the Social Science Research Council in New York writes:

> When Republicans won control of Congress in elections just a week later [after the signing of the Agreed Framework in 1994], unilateralists in the Republican Party denounced the deal as appeasement. Unwilling to challenge Congress, the Clinton administration shrank from implementation. Construction of the

---

to achieve peace and security on a nuclear-free Korean Peninsula. See www.kedo.org/pdfs/AgreedFramework.pdf.

9. 'Agreed Framework between the United States of America and the Democratic People's Republic of Korea' (21 October 1994), www.kedo.org.

10. *The Washington Post*, 20 October 2002.

first replacement reactor was slow to begin – it was supposed to be ready by 2003 but is three years behind schedule – and the heavy-fuel oil was not always delivered on schedule. Above all, Washington did little to improve relations with Pyongyang.[11]

What Sigal argues in this and other works is that North Korea is playing tit-for-tat: 'cooperation whenever Washington cooperated and retaliating when Washington reneged, in an effort to end enmity.'[12] Siegfried S. Hecker is an American nuclear weapons specialist who has investigated the North Korean nuclear programme and visited North Korean nuclear facilities like no other Western expert. In a report from 2006 he states that: 'It is essential for the United States to demonstrably address DPRK's security before there is any hope of denuclearization.'[13] In 2010 Hecker elaborated this by stating that: 'We found that Pyongyang was willing to slow its drive for nuclear weapons only when it believed the fundamental relationship with the United States was improving.'[14] And finally, in 2011 he elaborates further stressing that it is the insecurity that informs the regime's reactions, as well as the issue of normalization of relations (between the US and the North). These issues have to be addressed, and it is a process that will take years, says Hecker. He continues that what it takes is that 'you have to understand the people, you have to understand the history and the culture, in order to understand the politics, whether there

11. L.V. Sigal (2002) 'North Korea is No Iraq: Pyongyang's Negotiation Strategy', *Arms Control Today*, December, p. 8

12. Ibid., p. 9.

13. Siegfried S. Hecker (2006) 'Report on North Korean Nuclear Program', Center for International Security and Cooperation, Stanford University, p.4

14. Siegfried S. Hecker (2010) 'Lessons learned from the North Korean nuclear crises', *Dædalus* (winter) p. 54.

is any chance of coming to a resolution.'[15] It is particularly these observations on the dynamics of the relations between North Korea and the outside world that we find interesting. If the North Koreans are basically 'reactive' to whatever approach the international community chooses, then engaging in relations is certainly more conducive to dialogue than is confrontation.

This insight, as well as a close look at the results of the history of enmity between the two Koreas inspired Kim Dae-jung, the world-famous political-activist-turned-president of South Korea, to create his so-called Sunshine Policy. For a relatively short period of ten years – during the presidencies of Kim and his predecessor Roh – South Korea made strong efforts to end the enmity and change the direction of inter-Korean relations built up over the past 55 years. Much was achieved but, despite the fact that President Kim received the Nobel Peace Prize in 2000 for his lifelong fight for democracy and human rights including for his ongoing struggle to secure peace on the Korean Peninsula, the strategy was not continued when Lee Myung-bak of the conservative Grand National (now Saenuri) Party moved into the Blue House in the spring of 2008.

During the first stages, when the Sunshine Policy was the official South Korean strategy towards the North, it gained quite strong international support, illustrated by the peace prize and in particular by statements from the third Asia–Europe Meeting (ASEM) in Seoul in 2000 and the fourth meeting in Copenhagen in 2002. Under Kim Dae-jung's chairmanship, the 48 ASEM members 'welcomed the historic first inter-Korean summit held in June 2000 in Pyongyang and acknowledged the great significance of this event which has laid the foundation for

---

15. Siegfried S. Hecker (2011) in Google Tech Talks at Stanford University, March 28. Available at: (http://www.youtube.com/watch?v=VldRSI7Dc88).

the peace process on the Korean peninsula'.[16] Two years later, at the Copenhagen ASEM summit, the European and Asian state leaders still strongly supported 'the process of inter-Korean reconciliation and cooperation'.[17]

However, while the ASEM leaders at the Seoul Summit had welcomed 'the recent positive developments in relations between the DPRK and the United States',[18] with a new administration in Washington, the situation soon became entirely different. In January 2002, then US President George W. Bush termed North Korea, together with a small number of Muslim countries, the 'Axis of Evil'. Later he added another disparaging term: the 'Outpost of Tyranny'. As a result, relations between North Korea and the US went from bad to worse. Chung-in Moon, a South Korean political scientist and specialist on North Korea, writes that 'a deeply rooted distrust of North Korea, which was widely shared among key decision-makers in the Bush administration, blocked the chance for direct bilateral talks'.[19] That the distrust was mutual was clearly revealed later the same year.

Lost in Translation: the Failure of Cross-Cultural Communication

US intelligence reports in the summer of 2002 claimed that North Korea might have a secret, highly enriched uranium

---

16. Chairman's Statement of the Third Asia–Europe Meeting, Seoul, 20-21 October 2000. See http://www.consilium.europa.eu/uedocs/cms_data/docs/pressdata/en/er/Chairmans.doc.html.

17. ASEM 4 – Chairman's Statement. See www.aseminfoboard.org/summit-statement.html.

18. 'Seoul Declaration for Peace on the Korean Peninsula'. Located at www.aseminfoboard.org.

19. Chung-in Moon (2011) 'The Six party Talks and Implications for a Northeast Asia Nuclear Weapons Free Zone', Report presented at the East Asia Nuclear Security workshop in Tokyo, 11 November,. Available at http://nautilus.org/napsnet.

programme. The international community was alarmed. In October that year, US Assistant Secretary of State for East Asian and Pacific Affairs James Kelly paid a visit to the North Korean capital.[20] He confronted the North Koreans about their clandestine nuclear programme. His Northern counterparts reportedly responded that they had something even stronger than nuclear weapons. 'US analysts initially concluded that the North Korean delegation was alluding to chemical and biological weapons', and 'it took US officials weeks or months to clarify the meaning of the North Korean delegation's statement by speaking with foreign envoys [in Pyongyang] and the South Korean government'.[21] What, then, was the meaning of the North Korean statement? Not surprisingly, when interpreted within a North Korean political culture context, they had simply said something the gist of which was: as we stand united behind the direction of our leader, we constitute a fierce and undefeatable force, and as such we will reject any sort of aggression. The miscommunication between Kelly and the North Koreans is touched upon in a very interesting North Korean Foreign Ministry statement:

> In October 2002, special envoy Kelly, who visited Pyongyang, said that he had intelligence data on the highly enriched uranium program and threatened us by saying that if we did not present it not only DPRK–US relations but also DPRK–Japan and North–South relations will enter a catastrophic state. We were angered by the US side's extremely overt pressuring act that ignored not only our sovereignty but even the guests' etiquette to the host in the oriental culture. Thus our side clearly stated that we are entitled to possess even more powerful weapons than nuclear weapons to cope with the United

20. See www.nti.org/country-profiles/north-Korea/nuclear.
21. D.A. Pinkston and P.C. Saunders (2003) 'Seeing North Korea Clearly', *Survival*, vol. 45, no. 3, p. 82.

States' growing maneuvers to isolate and crush us and we did not even feel the need to bother to explain to the US side, the most hostile country, what they [the weapons] are.[22]

Although the North Koreans may use a form of communication unfamiliar to the outside world, it seems clear that there is more to this matter than just translation difficulties. Had the American delegation been more familiar with Korean culture (note the reference to oriental etiquette) and North Korean political rhetoric, this incipient crisis could have been avoided.

A dialogue across the ideological divide between North Korea and the US is obviously a challenging and highly sensitive affair. When the equally great cultural divide is added, the task is gigantic. Sensitivity to Korean ways is needed. After the visit by US envoy James Kelly, tensions between North Korea and the US became stronger, escalating towards a potential conflict.

At that point, recounts Chung-in Moon, 'China intervened and arranged a three-party talk among USA, North Korea and China in Beijing in April 2003. Strictly speaking, what China had in mind in arranging it was to create an opportunity for direct bilateral talks between Pyongyang and Washington within the three-party framework.'[23] China's efforts did not yield the expected outcome. While North Korea produced a concrete proposal, and China tried to mediate between the two adversaries, the US simply ignored the North's proposals. The American position was – and is – that the North has to start a

---

22. 'US Hostile Policy Disrupting 6-Way Talks', issued 8 October, 2004 by the Korean Central Broadcasting Station: Compiled and distributed by NTIS, US Dept. of Commerce/World News Connection. Available at www.dialogueselect.com.
23. Moon (2011) p. 5.

verifiable dismantling of its nuclear programme before the US will engage in a dialogue.[24]

Six party talks and the lack of mutual trust

The three-party talks developed later into six-party talks, adding South Korea, Japan and Russia. The stated aim of this dialogue is to find a peaceful solution to the security concerns triggered by the North Korean nuclear weapons programme.[25] The issues that dominate negotiations are that North Korea demands a security guarantee from the US side; the construction of two light-water nuclear reactors and the peaceful use of nuclear energy; trade normalization and diplomatic relations; and verifiable and irreversible disarmament.[26] Hitherto there have been five rounds of talks but no tangible results. So called breakthroughs were reported in 2005 and 2007, but each time, disagreement between North Korea and the US regarding the interpretation of what was agreed upon hindered materialization of the agreement.

If one were to try to locate one particular point between the parties in the six-party talks as a main reason for the lack of tangible results, it would have to be the different approaches to the types of agreements the parties may engage in and the requirements they are obliged to fulfil to keep the agreement. The US wants North Korea to give up its nuclear ambitions and accept a verifiable dismantling of the programme. This position is supported by Japan. North Korea on the other hand, argues for a step-by-step solution, where each party moves one step at a time in the agreed upon direction. This approach is supported by China, Russia and, until recently, also South Korea.

24. Ibid.
25. See http://en.wikipedia.org/wiki/Six-party_talks.
26. Ibid.

In the latest 'breakthrough' to date, the 2007 agreement, the text emphasizes *the need to develop mutual trust*: 'The Parties reaffirmed that they will take positive steps to increase mutual trust, and will make joint efforts for lasting peace and stability in Northeast Asia. The directly related parties will negotiate a permanent peace regime on the Korean Peninsula at an appropriate separate forum.'[27] So, aside from their different ideas on what the dialogue is about and how the parties concerned are supposed to keep to what they agree upon, the parties are aware of and have agreed on the need to improve mutual trust. While North Korea has maintained that its nuclear ambitions have always been and still are civilian, the world has been witness to the existence of a North Korean military programme due to the testing of a nuclear device in 2006, in 2009 and again in 2013. The US – and with it most of the Western world – are saying that the three nuclear tests have given the ultimate proof that North Korea cannot and should not be trusted. Another option, though, is to see North Korea's actions as basically relational. In 1994 the US considered a pre-emptive attack on the Yongbyon nuclear facility, and in 2004, then US Vice President Dick Cheney told a group of top officials: 'We don't negotiate with evil. We defeat it,'[28] and as a general threat, he added that *all options remain on the table*. North Korea may well, as suggested by Sigal, have wanted to keep weapons developed before the negotiations started as its ace in the hole, which it will not yield until it feels secure from US attack.[29] Today, ten years later, former US ambassador to South Korea and a leading expert on Korean issues, Donald Gregg, states: 'Kim is

27. See www.fmprc.gov.cn/eng/zxxx/t297463.htm.
28. L.V. Sigal (2006) 'Try Engagement for a Change', *Global Asia, The Debate*, Fall, p. 55
29. L.V. Sigal (2003) 'Negotiating with the North', *Bulletin of the Atomic Scientists*, Nov./Dec..

apparently showing his intent to develop his country's nuclear capabilities not as a threat, but as a deterrent.'[30] North Korea is insecure, the two main parties in the six-party talks stand worlds apart regarding what a dialogue covers and implies, and trust is at level zero.

The conflict seems unresolvable. Disagreements regarding the nuclear issue illustrate just how far apart the contending parties are. The human rights issue is as explosive as the nuclear one – here, too, the parties are worlds apart. Still, in this book we shall try to take up the human rights issue and reflect on what the social sciences can contribute.

Political Culture and Human Cognition Matter

Cross-cultural studies in psychology, sociology and political science relevant to the subject at hand show that the basic structures in people's mental maps are influenced by cultural traits. They also show that societal institutions and structures differ in operational technique according to the personnel who populate them. Moreover, they show that such fundamentals in politics as power and legitimacy are perceived differently within different political cultures, and that these differences often, but not always, follow political-geographical borders. Although such cultural differences are not static, the process of change can best be measured in decades, if not generations. In the short run, these differences are therefore to be reckoned with and taken seriously.

We generally assume that political actors in international relations perceive the world 'as it is' (that is, as *we* see it), and that possible misperceptions, if they occur, will be corrected within larger systems such as governmental agencies, interna-

---

30. Interview, the Hankyoreh, http://english.hani.co.kr/popups/print. hani?ksn=572838. Downloaded: 10.02.2013

tional organizations and diplomatic institutions. This view is, however, not at all supported by studies in social psychology, which in recent years have made important discoveries.[31] Their contribution is as simple as it is necessary: in short, the claim is that organizations, institutions and countries do not act; people act. And because this is the case, human cognition obviously matters – in foreign policy as well as in world politics.

If, according to volumes of psychological research, it is naïve to expect rational actors, what is then to be expected in a dialogue between Western governments on the one hand and the North Korean government on the other? Paul Watzlawick, psychologist and theoretician of communication found that *the belief that one's own view of reality is the only reality is the most dangerous of all delusions.*[32] What psychologists have found is that there is a universal tendency to overemphasize the influence of the external situation when explaining the behaviour of the self; we act as we do because of certain external reasons. In trying to explain the behaviour of others, it is common to overemphasize internal and dispositional factors: they act as they do because they are bad, aggressive, suspicious by nature, etc. This not only applies when trying to explain the negative actions of others: if the other, contrary to our expectations, acts positively, we tend to think that it is because certain characteristics of the situation have temporarily forced the other to be friendly. In this connection, another general finding holds that, if the other acts positively, one is inclined to attribute

31. C.R. Cooper and J. Denner (1998) 'Theories Linking Culture and Psychology: Universal and Community-Specific Processes', in *Annual Review of Psychology*, vol. 49, pp. 559–584; J.Y. Chiao, Zhang Li, and Tokiki Harada (2008) 'Cultural Neuroscience of Consciousness. From Visual Perceptions to Self-Awareness', in *Journal of Consciousness Studies*, vol. 15, no. 10–11, pp. 58–69.

32. Paul Watzlawick (1976) *How Real is Real? Confusion, Disinformation, Communication*. New York: Vintage Books, Random House, p. xiii.

this to one's own conduct and to believe that our actions have forced them to do so – that is, one overestimates one's own importance. These traits are all clearly present in the above-mentioned dialogues between North Korea and the US. One solution to this problem is to try to use empathy to understand North Korea's motives.

Is Empathy Warranted?

In an insightful article entitled 'Seeing North Korea Clearly', Saunders and Pinkston, two scholars from the Monterey Institute's James Martin Center for Nonproliferation Studies, advocate empathy.[33] The authors stress that one should not confuse empathy with sympathy: to understand reality as it is understood by others does not imply agreement. It is vital, however, to understand the world as viewed from Pyongyang in order to avoid sub-optimal solutions at best and inadvertent war at worst. Such an understanding is extremely important in order to be able to engage with North Korea in a constructive dialogue.

Empathy presupposes an ability to accommodate differences, and that the parties concerned – despite their differences – are able to establish bonds and build mutual trust. This should not be alien to any of the parties concerned, as the ability to put oneself in the shoes of the other is considered a virtue both in Christianity and in Buddhism, the main religions of the West and of East Asia respectively. The importance of trust in human relations is one of the major contributions of the social sciences in the twentieth century. This insight is also increasingly acknowledged in real-world politics. As already mentioned, in the joint statement of the 2007 breakthrough meeting of the six-party talks in Beijing, it was stated that '[t]he

---

33. Pinkston and Saunders (2003).

Parties reaffirmed that they will take positive steps to increase mutual trust …' (paragraph VI).[34]

One can hardly imagine, however, that mutual trust can be established without a certain level of acceptance between the parties concerned. The present relations between North Korea and the Western world are, as the example of the visit by US special envoy James Kelly showed, based on anything but trust. But as an approach based on empathy may prove to be the most creative and productive approach between adversaries, the search for a remedy is crucial. A point of departure for establishing better relations must then be to acknowledge the legitimacy of the other party and continue to stress the importance of understanding the background of their perceptions, expectations and actions. In the case of the North Korean mindset, it seems clear that the impact of more than half a century of isolation must have had psychological consequences and affected the North Korean understanding of reality and the surrounding world.

From Relative Success to Economic Collapse

The division of Korea and the subsequent war from 1950–53 totally destroyed relations between the two halves of the peninsula. During the ensuing Cold War, the regimes in Pyongyang and Seoul were each backed by one of the two competing military superpowers of that time, and each Korean regime used the threat of the other as part of their raison d'être thus developing in total isolation from each other. While military rule in South Korea was presented as liberal democracy, in the North the tradition-based leadership cult with its strong sense of broken nationalism was disguised as a 'people's democracy', that is, a communist dictatorship.

34. See www.fmprc.gov.cn/eng/zxxx/t297463.htm.

© Reuters

Serious efforts and lost opportunities

There are not many observations available to portray a North Korean leader, although several state leaders have dropped a word or two to the press after having met 'the hermit' himself in Pyongyang. Surprisingly the few statements that can be found giving accounts of the number one Kim in the North are quite positive. An observer not affected by a positive bias beforehand is Madeleine Albright, U.S. State Secretary under President Clinton. In her book *Madam Secretary: A Memoir* (2003), she has a full chapter on her October 2000 visit to Pyongyang: Inside the Hermit Kingdom, where she frankly states: 'We knew little about Kim, who was reputed to be an unworldly recluse, more interested in making and watching movies than in governing.' (462)

During her talks with the Hermit (who talked) she found out that he was well aware of the dreadful situation of his country (466), that he saw Sweden as having a better socialist system than his own(!) (ibid.), that he was ready to trade weapon programmes for economic assistance

(467). But 'What did he want? Above all, normal relations with the United States; that would shield his country from the threat he saw posed by American power and help him to be taken seriously in the eyes of the world.'(ibid.) Was Madeleine Albright fooled by a soft-spoken communist dictator, East Asian style? No, summing up her impressions from Pyongyang and her meetings with Kim Jong Il, she states that: 'One could not preside over a system as cruel as the DPRK's without being cruel oneself, but I did not think we had the luxury of simply ignoring him. He was not going to go away and his country, though weak, was not about to fall apart.'(ibid)

Back in Washington, discussions focused on the possibility to make a deal with the North Koreans. Albright and her staff believed so, 'The President himself was more than willing to make the trip...' (468). 'The best leverage we had was North Korea's desire for full normalization of relations.'(469) 'Kim Dae-jung strongly urged the President to go to Pyongyang, saying he was sure Kim Jong Il would want the trip to be a success (ibid.). But '[m]any in Congress and within the punditocracy opposed a summit because they feared a deal with North Korea would weaken the case for national missile defense'(ibid.). It was not this fear, however, or the uncertainty about success in Pyongyang, or the limited time left for the Clinton administration, but rather the crisis in the Middle East that stopped President Clinton from going to North Korea. (470) In January 19, 2001, a day before the President and his Secretary of State was to leave office they exchanged words on missed opportunities. Albright refers Clinton's reflections as follows: 'Fuming about all the time we had invested in Arafat, he said he wished he had taken the chance of going to North Korea instead of staying in Washington to make a final push on the Middle East.'(508).

Half a century spent as enemy powers vying for national legitimacy has formed the two halves of Korea. In the South, nationalism and a period of 'guided democracy' or rather benevolent but authoritarian leadership was gradually replaced by an American-oriented two-camp political system with what is effectively a presidential democracy. This notwithstanding, a traditional deference to great leaders is not alien to South Koreans, who seem somewhat torn between their support of democratic ideas, institutions and procedures, and an understanding of – and sometimes a craving for – paternalistic power and, hence, strong leadership.[35] The northern version of power, on the other hand has not been 'contaminated' by Western ideas. In the isolation enforced upon the country through an effective trade embargo and self-imposed by way of a proclaimed self-reliant development strategy, North Korea's political system has developed internally 'untainted' by any foreign ideas other than those accepted by the leadership.

During the colonial period, between 1910 and 1945, many patriotic and nationalistic Koreans fighting for their country's independence adopted socialism or communism as their ideology. Thus, indigenous Korean socialism already existed when the Soviet Red Army arrived in 1945. At the end of WWII, due to international agreements between the victorious powers, in particular the US and the Soviet Union, Korea was divided: the north was absorbed into the eastern communist sphere; the south into the western, liberal-democratic sphere. This temporary division became the sustained misfortune of the Korean people, who were thus deprived of their chance to develop a modern country after 35 years of colonial suppression under Japan.

---

35. Geir Helgesen developed this perspective in his *Democracy and Authority in Korea: The Cultural Dimension in Korean Politics.* Curzon Press, 1998.

A particular trait in the development of North Korea as a communist type of state was a strong emphasis on its independent position vis-à-vis the Soviet Union, China and others. The state ideology, Juche, was created around 1958, hailing national self-reliance and independence as core values. By doing it their way, the North Korean model was coloured more strongly by values and norms inherent in the pre-communist social system than by foreign ideological constructions à la Marx, Engels and Lenin. Initially, from an economic point of view, this indigenous system functioned well, partly due to its inner workings and partly because of strong support from the communist bloc (the CIA reported in 1972 that North Korea in several areas, notably energy and heavy industry, was ahead of South Korea).[36] As a result, North Korea commanded respect and goodwill abroad, especially in poorer and less-developed countries as well as among many students and intellectuals in South Korea.

The problem, however, has been an increasingly stagnating economy that was on the verge of total collapse in the late 1990s. Several attempts to boost production by mass campaigns after the collapse of Soviet communism and the fundamental changes in the Chinese economy, both strongly affecting North Korea, did not produce the expected outcome. In the mid- to late 1990s, large parts of the population suffered malnutrition and hunger. The consequences were grave and many paid with their lives. North Korea appealed for and received humanitarian aid, which must be seen as a new chapter in the country's relations with the outside world.

Around 2002 the leadership decided to embark on economic reforms, although cautiously, and without using the

---

36. CIA, *National Intelligence Estimate* (NIE) 42, 14.2–72, no. 288: 'The Two Koreas'.

concept 'reforms' directly, but instead a more neutral term – *adjustments*. Local markets, which seem to have been initiated locally, were now endorsed centrally. Although markets were downscaled a few years later, they had come to stay. The energy situation remained precarious, and as a consequence agricultural production was far below expectations. In 2008 and 2009 a relatively good harvest was reported. Markets were now allowed back in full scale. The energy situation was also somewhat better, as a number of new hydropower stations were opened. Frequent visitors to North Korea claim that people in the cities now seem to have more freedom to manage their daily lives, an observation we tend to support and will take up later.

Although the economy seems to have improved, not much improvement has been seen in the countryside. The change from the paternal state that provided welfare to all to a state that hardly could provide for itself and its immediate supporters has most likely contributed to undermining the trust between the people and the system. In general, therefore, the current economic crisis is seen as a state of affairs that will continue until a clear and sustainable reform strategy is implemented and starts to produce tangible positive results.

There are obviously different ideas and strategies among the North Korean elites regarding 'adjustments',[37] as will be made clear in the proceeding chapters. One might think that such differences would be outside of external influence and that the question of whether reformers or hardliners gain the upper hand in Pyongyang is ultimately an internal struggle upon which we have no effect. In a relational perspective this is not necessarily so: the outside world can stimulate the one or the other faction by choosing a tough or a lenient approach.

---

37. North Korean bureaucrats prefer the term 'adjustments' to 'reforms' when discussing economic and societal development strategies.

A huge problem, however, is that the North Korean leadership is not only unable to provide for its own population, it is also depicted as the worst thinkable political entity, governing a country populated by suppressors and victims only. Hence, normalcy has no place in the international community's picture of North Korea, a country with a population of 23 million. By condemning the country's dictatorship from a democratic position while ignoring the North Korean population, the West is contributing to rendering the people at large irrelevant. Our advice here is that instead of contributing to North Korea's further isolation, we make relations and engage in dialogue. But how should we address questions such as human, individual and collective rights in a country as singular as North Korea?

The Individual and Society: a Korean Model?

When dealing with human rights, there are strong reasons for sensitivity to Korean ways. David Steinberg, a long-term observer of the Korean scene, writes: '[I]n societies, such as Korea, in which individualism is not held as sacrosanct, a strong tradition of shared values, relationships, and social expectations, together with the acceptance of the political legitimacy of a particular regime, may create forces toward ideological conformity and orthodoxy that have both positive and negative attributes.'[38] From a Western viewpoint, one may be inclined to dwell on the negative effects, especially in the case of North Korea, but foreign observers should be able to contextualize things more objectively from a historical perspective. In Steinberg's words, 'perceived external threats, in the Korean cases from either the left or the right in the instances

---

38. D. Steinberg (1998) 'Human Rights in North Korea: a Reinterpretation', in C.I. Moon (ed.), *Understanding Regime Dynamics in North Korea*, Seoul: Yonsei University Press, pp. 241–242.

of the South and the North, produce a sense and manifestation of nationalism that encourage the subjugation of individual or group concerns to the common, threatened, weal'.[39]

One may find the social dynamics described by Steinberg quite negative, undemocratic and clearly against the human rights perspective. Nevertheless, until recently such social rules were entrenched in Korea, both South and North, and especially in the northern part of the peninsula they still are. Western observers should be careful not to employ their own worldview as the sole determinant when observing and evaluating events in Korea. Individualism, civil society and the hard-won independence of the individual in relation to the state are not necessarily universal ideals. The role of the state versus society is different in both Korea and in East Asia as a whole from what we are used to. This means that the state has a much more active role and intervenes in social as well as in-dividual affairs more than is normally accepted in the West. In Korea this is built on extensive historical precedence. 'Koreans in both North and South', writes Steinberg, 'rule on the basis of perceived moral authority, however defined, and that authority is likely to continue to give the leaders the motivation to act paternally. And the people to accept such actions from a regime that is regarded as politically legitimate.'[40]

Politics and Traditional Korean Culture

In order to understand the peculiar North Korean system it is important to realize that the long period in almost total isola-tion has formed the way in which leaders and followers coexist – the way the individual versus the group is perceived, how people at large view the world outside their own country, and

39. Ibid., p. 242.
40. Ibid., p. 248.

how they see their own role in society. A lot of traits attributed to the political Juche ideology and rationalized within that context were actually already deeply rooted in the traditional culture. Examples are the emphasis on the collective before the individual, the patriarchally based leadership and the perception of the society as an extended family. When people are virtually cultivated to see the leader as their father, his hardship and failures (which of course are theirs as well) will not necessarily make them turn against him. The results untold, ordinary people tend to believe that whatever the leader chooses to do, it is for the sake of the people, as was assumed in the traditional paternalistic family. In his 'Human Needs, Human Rights, and Regime Legitimacy' the prominent American-Korean scholar Han S. Park writes: 'The ordinary people submit themselves voluntarily to the authority because they are not accorded with alternative choices or oriented toward doubting the virtue of the leadership'.[41] Are they then blind to the dire reality of their daily life? Do they not feel their own hunger and discomfort? According to Park, 'The people in North Korea are sufficiently informed and socialized with the notion that their economic difficulty is due to the hostile international community and natural disasters for which their regime is not liable'.[42]

In the particular North Korean version of tradition-based 'communism', political socialization has been designed to imbue a system of mass belief reminiscent of that often found in sectarian and fanatical religions. A basic goal of the mass belief system has been the creation of charismatic leadership. This again is based on a traditional patriarchal social and moral ideology informed by the teaching of Confucius, with which

41. H.S. Park, in C.I. Moon (ed.) (1998) *Understanding Regime Dynamics in North Korea: Contending Perspectives and Comparative Implications.* Seoul: Yonsei University Press, p. 234.

42. Ibid., p. 225.

the Korean people were imbued throughout the Yi Dynasty (1392–1910), when Confucianism was the state ideology as well as a dominant social morality. The selective utilization by the political elite of certain aspects of this widespread and deep-rooted creed may explain the durability of the political ideology, even beyond the material collapse of the system. The present North Korean worldview is to be understood as the result of a cleverly designed combination of political socialization and political propaganda, both based on a total information monopoly. The effect is that it sustains the support for the given system. The political socialization, an area of top priority in North Korea, has been emphasizing this Confucian-communist view without any challenge from alternative ideas or views for 50 years. Nowadays, of course, this education and the resulting political culture is totally outdated and has no place in the contemporary world but its result, a particular mental state, lingers on. Professor Park has with deep insight into the psychology of the North Korean people explained this:

> Without interruption in the progression of socialization for several decades, Juche has been able to deeply penetrate and assimilate itself into the mass belief system. The degree of rigidity and saliency of beliefs may have reached a point at which external disturbances may not easily cause psychological dissonance.[43]

This is not to say that all North Koreans think alike – on the contrary, we want to stress that among North Korean bureaucrats there are different opinions on the question of opening up to the international community. Yet what is described above is important when Western governments try to understand the background of the *perceptions, expectations*

---

43. Han S. Park (2002) *North Korea. The Politics of Unconventional Wisdom.* Boulder, Colorado: Lynne Rienner, p.63.

and *actions* of North Korean government officials. Without an understanding of what basically informs the way one's counterpart understands reality and perceives the world, a dialogue can hardly produce results that aim at changing relations between those very partners.

Unfortunately, Western media have no patience to seek reasons and causes and they seem to be doing what they can to sustain an extremely negative and bleak picture of North Korea by disregarding the historical and cultural background of that country.

Effects of this Bleak Picture

Few countries, possibly no others in our contemporary world, are branded as negatively as North Korea. 'North Korean conditions' are almost universally used to depict the worst possible state of affairs. And more than that, the apparently 'formidable' military force of North Korea is used as a strong reason for the West to stand by the US in its global defence strategies.[44] North Korea has long occupied a position as a pariah state. No claim seems too horrific to be believed, if it is said to be happening in North Korea. During the periods of hunger in the 1990s, cannibalism was reported and, since it happened in that country, it was not only cannibalism that was reported – it was also said that the human flesh that was being consumed came from children.

Recently, the transfer of the dictator's mantle from father to (third) son preoccupied world media to an astonishing degree. Nothing substantial was then reported about the

---

44. The Minister of Defence in Denmark at the time, Søren Gade, expressed strong concerns about the nuclear programmes in North Korea and Iran, claiming that the alarming developments in these two countries were the reason that Denmark joined the US anti-missile shield program. *Information*, 25 July 2007.

next-generation leader in Pyongyang, but this did not stop the media from continuous speculation. Then, the rumours from the intelligence world concerning the designated leader of the Pyongyang regime claimed that he had been observed during his childhood years enjoying inflicting pain on insects and animals. In this regard, it seems appropriate to recall a statement about intelligence by the former US ambassador to South Korea, Donald Gregg, who before that important post was head of the CIA activities in South Korea and later became National Security Advisor: 'I refer to North Korea as the longest-running intelligence failure in the history of US espionage.'[45]

The problem with the often monotonous media focus on negative and critical stories from North Korea is that the general picture of the country turns out worse than necessary, creating obstacles for the establishment of contacts and dialogue. By demonizing the country, the population of North Korea is basically being divided into two very unequal groups, the crude oppressors and the poor oppressed. The first group is obviously small, and commands an extensive repressive apparatus; the second, then, is the majority of the population, who have no way to influence their life situation short of fleeing the country. Such a crude picture, repeatedly transmitted through media outlets with no space left for alternatives, means that even plain descriptions of daily life activities in North Korea risk being seen as pro-regime propaganda. Although terms such as 'axis of evil' and 'outpost of tyranny' are less frequently used now than they were some years ago, the North has never escaped its extremely negative image. This directly affects relations with

---

45. Interview with Donald Gregg in *Frontline*, 20 February 2003, seen at www.pbs.org/wgbh/pages/frontline/shows/kim/interviews/gregg.html.

the outside world, not least the likelihood of a constructive dialogue on human rights.

The Aborted Human Rights Dialogue

In 2001 the EU engaged in a human rights dialogue with North Korea. There had been some meetings in Brussels and also in Pyongyang before the EU at a UN human rights session in Geneva proposed a resolution condemning the human rights situation in the North. The resolution was adopted in April 2003. North Korea immediately pulled out of the dialogue process.

Shortly after the collapse of the dialogue we met with representatives from both the EU side and the North Korean Ministry of Foreign Affairs, which revealed a profound difference in how this event was perceived. The EU representatives justified the condemnation by pointing to the fact that, according to available information, the human rights situation in North Korea was critical. These representatives said directly that it would be impossible for elected politicians in Europe not to support a declaration condemning North Korea *in light of the very negative press coverage of the country.*[46]

From the opposite side of the table, the reality looked different. For the North Korean regime to engage in a dialogue with Western powers took guts. After long and difficult internal deliberations, it had been decided that it was reasonable to meet the EU in a human rights dialogue, even if this was the ballgame of the other, and particularly as the North Koreans had to prepare themselves for criticism. They prepared for that, but they were not ready for dire condemnation. That was too much for the leadership in Pyongyang, and, from their perspective, unacceptable, as then it was no longer a dialogue

---

46. Personal communication, Pyongyang, 2004.

but a relationship between a superior and an inferior power, a picture to which the regime is allergic based on historical experiences. Whether the North Korean perspective is seen as right or wrong has no bearing in this connection; here we are dealing with the attitude and behaviour of the country's elite in their relationship to the outside world.

A senior North Korean official wondered how the EU could propose a dialogue and initiate a condemnation at the same time:

> They should have been aware that some people on our side are in favour of a dialogue, while others reject it. The EU-sponsored condemnation of the human rights situation in North Korea was a welcome support to those who reject any dialogue.[47]

One younger government official said that, if the whole world is preoccupied with the human rights situation in North Korea, there should be a dialogue on this issue. In his opinion it was too defensive to refuse such a dialogue because it would only make it easier for enemies of North Korea to paint the darkest possible picture of the situation in the country. Referring to his colleagues, he claimed that those belonging to the younger generation generally seek more openness and want to meet the challenges from the outside world, while the old guard is not at all keen on this – they claim that it is tantamount to 'playing with fire.' He described the human rights dialogue with the EU as an example of how the younger and older generations disagree:

> After the collapse of that dialogue, we, the younger officials, were criticized for having put ourselves and also them (the older generation) in a weak or even impossible position.[48]

47. Ibid.
48. Ibid.

The conclusion of this younger official was that the actions of the EU, in this case, benefited the hardliners who are fighting openness and change. Then, how can the North Korean regime be dealt with? How can one enter into involvement with North Korea without fortifying the existing system's most conservative forces? How could North Korea be approached and what should be avoided? First, we suggest looking more closely at North Korea's interactions and experiences within the UN Human Rights regime.

CHAPTER 2

North Korea's Interaction with the UN Human Rights Regime, 2000–11

*I*n the previous chapter, we contend that the West generally lacks knowledge and understanding of North Korea's
relations to the outside world, the reasoning of its
decision-makers, and thus how a dialogue on human rights
can be facilitated. It goes without saying that the North Korean
elite also has an inadequate level of information on and understanding of the West. The point of departure for a dialogue is
therefore weak and, unless this fundamental flaw is remedied,
the likelihood of a collapse of new attempts at dialogue is im-
minent. Yet, dialogue and interaction on human rights have
been tried, specifically through the UN Human Rights regime,
to which we will now turn.

North Korea has involved itself in the international human
rights system since the early 1980s, even though the country
first gained a seat in the UN in 1991. This interaction runs
along several tracks that are interrelated and, in their totality,
present a sad picture of blocked communications and lack of
results. The expressed intention from both sides is a constructive communication and mutual support but the reality is the

exact opposite: unending talks at cross-purposes for more than a decade now.

The human rights regime of the United Nations consists of a web of bureaucracies and mechanisms relating to each other and aimed at, on the one hand, furthering the implementation of human rights treaties, on the other, monitoring compliance with these standards – that is to say, investigating violations and imposing sanctions. These two functions can easily come into conflict with each other, as we shall see in the following. The conflict is inherent in the system and does not specifically pertain to the relations between the North Korean leadership and the UN treaty bodies or specialized agencies but to relations between all states and the UN system.

The most important channels of interaction between the UN human rights system and a member state are:

- Ratification of human rights treaties and periodic reporting to the matching committees.

- Since 2006, examination of member states under the mechanism of the Universal Periodic Review (UPR), under which all countries' human rights record are examined every fourth year.

- Participation in the annual sessions in the main body, the Commission on Human Rights (CHR), which in 2006 was replaced by the Human Rights Council (HRC).[1] The Human Rights Council conducts the Universal Periodic Review; it can adopt resolutions on specific countries and establish so called Special Procedures.

- The Special Procedures involve appointment of a Special Rapporteur (SR) – an independent academic or a working

---

1. The Human Rights Council is an inter-governmental body within the UN system subsidiary to the General Assembly. It is made up of 47 states on a rotating basis. The HRC is responsible for strengthening the promotion and protection of human rights around the globe.

group scrutinizing human rights protection in one country/ region or investigating a topic related to systematic violations of human rights across countries.

North Korea has been engaged in all these kinds of interaction and the processes will be discussed below one by one. There are clear links and even trade-offs between the different avenues. Ratification of treaties or conventions and reporting to treaty bodies is the 'normal' means of interaction, as is examination by the committees and, after 2006, undergoing the Universal Periodic Review. These mechanisms are equal for all. Every country in the world must interact with the UN system in that way; it could be called 'support implementation'. However, the international human rights system has certain other measures available for special cases in which the 'system' (or the most powerful members of the system) finds them necessary in order to guarantee the most basic rights for the population of a country or a region, or to solve some special problem areas such as 'involuntary disappearances'. These Special Procedures, as they are aptly called, single out a country as a perpetrator of human rights violations to a greater degree than other countries and, by their very nature, they are seen as an exercise in degradation – or even punishment for what can be viewed as an unwanted political system or behaviour. Here we call them 'investigation of violations'. The two tracks, on the one hand to promote the implementation of human rights and on the other the monitoring process, are also viewed by the countries subjected to Special Procedures, or those threatened with subjection to them, in light of the dichotomy of cooperation vs. confrontation. In the case of North Korea in the following analysis we shall see how these two 'tracks' of the same system influence each other so that activities on one track destroy the foundation for success on the other.

Human Rights Treaties: North Korean Ratification and Compliance

Four of the six core conventions have been ratified by North Korea: the International Covenant on Civil and Political Rights (ICCPR) and the International Covenant on Economic, Social and Cultural Rights (ICESCR) in 1981 – even though the country at that time was not a member of the UN. The Convention on the Rights of the Child (CRC, also called the Children's Convention) was ratified in 1990 and the Convention for Elimination of All Discrimination against Women (CEDAW, also called the Women's Convention) in 2001. Few of the obligatory reports[2] have been submitted and, with one exception none since 2002. A report on children's rights was submitted in 2007, but for the other reports due in 2008, 2009 and 2010 respectively, none have been submitted. Compliance with the CRC has been rather consistent and has followed the rules irrespective of conflicts between the UN and the North Korean regime, while compliance with the other treaties has not. The CRC is often regarded as the least politically sensitive convention as protection of children is considered an issue everyone can support.[3] Cooperation on issues such as children, disabled persons and so on is also often regarded as the most viable means of engaging the North Korean leadership in a discussion on human rights issues.[4]

The delay in submission of reports is, however, not really exceptional. Many countries, especially the poor ones, have difficulties living up to the demands of the UN system. There

---

2. Each convention is implemented through a committee, requiring a comprehensive report every four or five years.
3. The CRC has been ratified by all (192) members of the UN, which is by far the highest score for any treaty.
4. Personal notes from conference in Chatham House, London, 2–3 December 2010.

Table 1: History of North Korean Compliance with Treaty Obligations

Conven-tion	Ratified	1st report	2nd report	3rd report	4th report	Concluding observations
ICCPR	1981	1983	2000	Due 2004	Due 2009	1984–2001
ICESCR	1981	1983–89	2002	Due 2008		2004 and before
CEDAW	2001	2002	Due 2006	Due 2010		2005 and before
CRC	1990	1996	2002	2007	2007	2003-04-09

are nine committees – and North Korea is responsible to four of them through ratification – which all expect a comprehensive report every fourth year. Writing such a report is a time-consuming and difficult task, as it means that the necessary statistics and information must be available, that different ministries must work together and deliver data, and that social organizations – if there are any – must be heard, among other things. All in all, it is a cumbersome process usually coordinated by a special office, which is probably understaffed and overburdened, in the Ministry of Foreign Affairs. We know little about how the reporting process in North Korea is organized,[5] but it seems the efforts to draft reports have been stalled for quite a while. Table 1 (above) provides a summary of North Korea's compliance with its treaty obligations.

The North Korean state reports of the early 2000s follow the prescribed pattern, commenting on the conventions paragraph by paragraph. The content basically states that everything is fine: the legal guarantees are in place and citizens' human rights are fully protected; every adult is provided with a job by the state 'in accordance with their wises and skills'; all citizens enjoy social security; all citizens are equal before the law; court hearings are open to the public 'on principle'; and

---

5. For CRC and CEDAW we know that the government has set up National Coordination Committees including officials from the relevant ministries and law enforcement agencies. CRC/C/65/Add.24 par. 16 and CEDAW/C/PRK/1, par. 4.

so on. There are no sections on problems or challenges except for the often-repeated information that 'successive natural disasters from 1994 and the collapse of the socialist market in the early 1990s ... brought about unexpected difficulties in ... various ... sectors of the national economy'.[6] The consequences of these 'unexpected difficulties', however, are not hidden. Alarming figures are published, for example, a fall in average life expectancy for females from 78 years in 1991 to 71 years in 1999. The mortality rate for children under the age of five rises from 27 in 1993 to 48 in 1999. Grain production falls from 9.1 million tons in 1990 to 3.3 million in 2000. Thus, one can say that the hard facts of the human rights situation in the 1990s are not concealed, even though the economic and social system is characterized as sound and generous towards the welfare of the population.

The submission of a report is followed by discussions (or an 'examination') between the committee in charge of the specific convention and a delegation from the member state. The committee will subsequently issue so-called 'concluding observations' containing recommendations from the Committee to the member state after having read the report and heard the answers from the delegation.

In the concluding observations on North Korea from the different committees, there are certain recurring elements pointing at alleged systemic weaknesses in the North Korean system. Even though each convention treats different areas and has different target groups, a recommendation concerning health and more specifically malnutrition appears in all of them. Even in the recommendations from the Human Rights Committee in 2001 – dealing with civil and political rights – there is a clause on the food situation, referring directly to

---

6.   E/1990/6/Add.35, par. 66.

article 6 on the right to life.[7] Thus the food situation in North Korea is very high on the agenda of the human rights system as such. The mentioned concluding observation can be said to accuse the North Korean government of killing people; obviously a serious violation. In relation to the food situation, the obligation to seek international assistance if a state is not able to live up to its obligations is stressed many times. Additional recurring comments are related to occurrences of torture and other forms of violence including use of the death penalty and public executions, to the need for reliable and systematic data collection aiming at following development over time, to the urgency of allocating sufficient budgets to the different areas, and to the difficulties in travelling into and out of the country and the practice of severe punishment for crossing the border. An unusual concern is expressed in the concluding observations on the Children's Convention, namely an appeal to avoid institutionalization of children unless it is absolutely necessary and to strengthen the role of the parents.[8] The Children's Convention Committee is concerned about the 'significant number of children who are placed in institutions'. There is also a call for restraint in militarization of children, 'particularly in schools'.[9] In general, the concluding observations also express the fear that security concerns override the protection of human rights.

Certain comments in the history of reporting support a North Korean claim discussed below, namely that the relation with the treaty bodies from 2000 to 2002 was developing positively. For one thing, the fact that state reports on all four of the conventions to which North Korea is a party were submitted in

---

7.   CCPR A/56/40 (2001), par. C12.
8.   CRC/C/PRK/CO/4, par. 37.
9.   Ibid., par. 59.

the period 2000–2002. This shows a degree of conformity to treaty obligations never seen before or since. In the 2001 concluding observations, the Human Rights Committee praises the state party for sending a strong delegation for the examination composed of representatives of different state agencies and for expressing a readiness to continue the dialogue with the committee after the examination.[10] This is in contrast to the sarcastic remark made in a concluding observation from 1987, in which the Committee on Social, Economic and Cultural Rights – apart from complaining about the meagre report – says that 'many members felt that the reference to "a paradise on earth" seemed somewhat inappropriate'.[11] The North Korean delegation answered that 'the word "paradise" was simply utilized in order to make a contrast between the present situation and the doomed past, when the people were subjected to feudalism, slavery, servitude and foreign exploitation and domination'.[12] No more references to a 'paradise on earth' can be found in the later reports from Pyongyang. Moreover, the International Covenant on Civil and Political Rights Committee in 2001 appreciates, among other things, that domestic laws had been translated and made available; that the number of criminal offences carrying the death penalty had been reduced; that the Women's Convention had been ratified; and that exchange visits between families from the two Koreas had taken place on several occasions.

The Human Rights Council

In spite of its disagreements with the human rights system since 2002, the government of North Korea submitted a report to

---

10. CCPR A/56/40 (2001), par. A2.
11. CESCR E/1987/28, par. 268.
12. Ibid., par. 270.

undergo the Universal Periodic Review as scheduled in August 2009 and the review was held in December the same year. The final report from the working group[13] came out on 4 January 2010 and was, together with responses from the North Korean government, adopted as part of the report from the following annual session of the Human Rights Council held 1–23 March 2010 in Geneva. According to procedure, the country makes a report, which is then published. All the other countries can then pose questions during the review itself, following a fixed procedure called an 'interactive dialogue'. The country then responds to the questions and all questions and answers are collected and adopted as the outcome of the Universal Periodic Review at a session of the Human Rights Council.

In the national report from 2009, the North Korean government uses the first 14 out of 20 pages to describe how everything in North Korea is arranged strictly in accordance with international standards and, concerning international co-operation, how 'invitations were extended to the delegations of the Amnesty International, International Association against Torture and the Committee on the Rights of the Child and the team of Special Rapporteurs of the Commission on Human Rights on violence against women'.[14] The rest of the report is dedicated to 'obstacles and challenges to the protection and promotion of human rights'. These obstacles are, first, the hostile policies of the United States, second, the 'anti-DPRK campaigns, including adoption of 'human rights resolutions' at the United Nations, and third, the dissolution of the socialist market and natural disasters.[15] If the order expresses a priority,

---

13. A 'troika' of rapporteurs is selected to facilitate a review, in this case: Mexico, Norway and South Africa (A/HRC/13/13, psr. 2).
14. A/HRC/WG.6/6/PRK/1, par. 76.
15. Ibid., par. 79–91.

foreign relations are seen by the Pyongyang leadership as the most important obstacles to improved protection of human rights in the nation. Considerable space is given to the resolutions:

> [T]he 'resolutions' are the root source of mistrust and confrontation, and the impediments to international cooperation (par. 85). ... [T]he very impediments in the way of materializing this cooperation are the above-mentioned 'resolutions', which are thoroughly politicized and selective. Selective attack and cooperation are incompatible (par. 86).

During the Universal Periodic Review event itself in December 2009, no less than 52 countries took the floor and posed questions. Many countries balanced positive comments with critical questions. For example, Brazil commended North Korea's participation in the Universal Periodic Review process and at the same time expressed concern about alleged executions in political detention camps. The North Korean delegation came up with the expected answers: citizens enjoy absolute freedom of expression, assembly, religion; people are not classified into categories and discriminated accordingly; political prisoners do not exist; the issue of malnutrition is a thing of the past, and so on. Some countries, like Cuba (but not China!), agreed with North Korea that the country had wrongfully been imposed upon with a Special Rapporteur and was a 'victim of imperialist aggressive policies' while a number of countries urged the Pyongyang leadership to invite the Special Rapporteur on a visit there.[16] Thus, the consideration of the outcome of the Universal Periodic Review,[17] which in some ways can be compared to the concluding observations,

16. A/HRC/13/L.10.
17. The outcome of the UPR is adopted as part of the report from the following annual session of the HRC, in this case the 13th session, held 1–23 March 2010 in Geneva.

namely the response of the UN system to the self-appreciation
of a member state, contains all the usual criticisms of human
rights violations in North Korea as well as the usual defence
by the leadership, including the claim that the 'resolutions'
obstruct full cooperation with the UN human rights regime,
consequently harming the North Korean citizens' enjoyment
of human rights. The pattern of the ongoing fight about the
'resolutions' unfolding below repeats itself: the outside world
insists on criticizing North Korea and the North Korean leadership insists that nothing is wrong.

Special Rapporteur: Communication Obstructed

Looking at Table 1, it appears that the process of interaction
lost momentum after 2002, when the relationship between
North Korea and the international community went from bad
to worse. Several actions from 2003 onwards strengthened the
confrontational approach on the side of the UN, as is discussed
in the following section. On January 19, 2011, the permanent
representative of the DPRK to the United Nations Office at
Geneva, So Se Pyong, addressed a letter to the president of the
Human Rights Council,[18] in which he stated that his country
'categorically and resolutely' rejected the Special Rapporteur,
who was to give his report to the sixteenth session of the Human
Rights Council scheduled to take place in February. The letter
refers back to similar protests in 2007, 2008, 2009 and 2010; the
wording in these letters is practically the same. The letter could
also have mentioned a letter from February 2005 declaring its
non-recognition of a resolution from 2004, where the mandate of
the Special Rapporteur was decided upon. This move was never
accepted in Pyongyang, which accused it of being 'an extreme
manifestation of politicization, selectivity and double standards

18. A/HRC/16/G/2.

in the area of human rights'[19] – and these same arguments for refusing to recognize the mandate have been used in all later reactions from the North Korean representative. Between 2005 and 2011, the Special Rapporteur has submitted twelve reports to the General Assembly – almost two per year – and the North Korean permanent representative has responded seven times with repudiations and accusations. For more than five years, the process has consisted of the same exchange of accusations and counter-attacks; each side using exactly the same weapons in an endless battle over names and words.

The main complaint from the North Korean side is that in 2003, the US, Japan and the European Union, without notice and proper consultations, tabled a resolution on the human rights situation in North Korea and got it adopted in the Commission of Human Rights. At that time, a dialogue between North Korea and the EU allegedly was at 'an excellent phase', according to the personal recollections of one of the authors in the introduction. North Korea 'was involved in various activities of cooperation with international human rights mechanisms, including, in particular, the human rights treaty bodies'.[20] The main argument for tabling the resolution from the opposite side was concern about 'reports of systemic, widespread and grave violations of human rights in the Democratic People's Republic of Korea' in a number of areas and the fact that 'the authorities of the Democratic People's Republic of Korea have not created the necessary conditions to permit the international community to verify these reports in an independent manner'.[21]

A birds-eye view of the time-line at this moment reminds us that Madeleine Albright visited Pyongyang in October 2000;

---

19. A/65/391, par 29 and 30.
20. A/HRC/16/G/2.
21. E/CN.4/RES/2003/10.

the EU–North Korea human rights dialogue was prepared the year after at about the same time that the North Korean leadership moved towards economic reform. Then came the Bush doctrine defining North Korea as part of an 'Axis of Evil' in early 2002, and the US National Security Strategy followed in September. Drastic fluctuations in a short period of time relations between North Korea and the rest of the world were reflected on the human rights scene.

By the time of the fateful resolution, the channels of communication seemed to be seriously obstructed, and the appointment of the Special Rapporteur was doomed from the very beginning. However, the newly appointed Special Rapporteur, Vitit Muntharbon, in his first report from January 2005, describes his initial steps upon having received the assignment thus:

> [I]n September 2004, I spent one week in Geneva meeting with key actors, and I was pleased to be received by the representatives of the Democratic People's Republic of Korea in Geneva, although in my capacity as an academic rather than as Special Rapporteur. The meeting was cordial and constructive, and I look forward to further meetings in future.[22]

And later:

> The process adopted by this Special Rapporteur is based upon a constructive step-by-step approach, working progressively to promote and protect human rights in the country in a fair, balanced and independent manner.[23]

He continues by expressing his intent to serve as a 'catalyst for change', a 'humble change agent', and he looks forward to visiting the country, though 'to date, no invitation has been forthcoming'. He would have to wait a long time – in fact, no

22. E/CN.4/2005/34, par. 4.
23. Ibid., par. 5.

invitation was sent during his period of service, which, following the rules, expired in 2010. This initial optimism on the part of the rapporteur stands in sharp contrast to the attitude of the leadership in the country he set out to investigate. As mentioned above, only one month after the report of his 'cordial and constructive' meeting with the North Korean delegation, Pyongyang issued a strong condemnation and repudiation of the entire foundation for his mission:

> The resolution, as initiated by the European Union, is based on political motivations, taking sides with the United States policy of hostility against the DPRK and, therefore, has nothing to do with genuine promotion and protection of human rights.[24]

The regime goes one step further, declaring that the resolution is a 'fundamental obstacle' to any technical cooperation with the Office of the High Commissioner for Human Rights, which aim is also stated in the resolution. However, it is promised that:

> In the absence of any resolution against DPRK, the technical cooperation in the area of human rights would be realized spontaneously.[25]

Thus, the attempt to set up a human rights dialogue between North Korea and the European Union and, in fact, any discussion of human rights, ended with the resolution of April 2003. The same conclusion appears in talks with North Korean diplomats seven years later, as we shall come back to in Chapter 4 of this book. The North Korean government interprets the resolutions in the UN human rights system as hostile and confrontational actions, causing the North Korean leadership to reject offers of cooperation.

---

24. E/CN.4/2005/G/13.
25. Ibid.

No government wants to be criticized publicly in UN organs and other member states have reacted in the same way. The process of conferring with a party while simultaneously discrediting it within the same organizational framework (the UN human rights system) has, as this example shows, not proved very effective. The perceptions of the parties involved in the dialogue process are well documented in public statements and the temporal link between resolutions and cooperation projects establishes the fact that, following upon resolutions, little cooperation ensues. A basic conclusion of this study must then be that cooperation and contact strengthen opportunities for making an impact on the party with which one is dealing. The argument is not that criticism from the outside has no effect at all or must not take place. The problem is rather whether the same institution or organ can do both.

Thus, establishing a constructive and sustainable human rights dialogue with North Korea does not come easily and, as the above shows, requires a careful approach by both sides. The trade-off between cooperation and confrontation is well established and must be calculated into any decision to discredit a single country. The same trade-off can be seen in the case of the EU–China human rights dialogue, where 'constructive involvement' was also initiated under the precondition that no resolution against China would be put on the table.[26] In the following chapter we take a look at that particular process – and although its successes so far are relatively limited – it might offer some advice that can be utilized in the North Korea case.

---

26. Katrin Kinzelbach and Hatla Thelle (2011) 'Talking Human Rights to China: An Assessment of the EUs Approach', in *The China Quarterly*, no. 205, pp. 60–79.

CHAPTER 3

Lessons from the Human Rights Dialogue with China

*I*n the previous chapter, we described how encounters between nations on human rights issues take place within the UN framework. International efforts to promote protection of human rights in a particular country, however, can also be set in motion outside of this regime through multi- or bilateral exchanges of opinion, cooperative projects or promises of support by other means. History has shown that the different approaches are intertwined so that cooperation on human rights protection outside the UN system by the parties will or can be linked to behaviour within the UN system and vice versa. We have seen that North Korea declares that it is willing to cooperate and receive help from other countries if these actors do not support UN resolutions and other perceived hostile measures. In the case of China, the same mechanism is at play.

In the following, we will show how a precondition for participation in multi- and bilateral activities concerning human rights in China has been that the potential partner countries do not support critical resolutions in the UN.

Human Rights Dialogues Outside the UN System

The so-called human rights dialogues are one type of interaction utilized instead of – or concurrently with – confrontation within the UN system. Such dialogues can be structured in numerous ways and have so far had varying results. In certain cases, cooperative projects seeking to promote human rights across borders take the following form: an institution in one country signs an agreement with an institution in another country to provide financial aid for activities aimed at improving protection in specific areas. In some contexts, these projects are labelled 'technical assistance', for example within the office of the high commissioner for human rights. On the bilateral level, they are extensively used as development projects or partnerships. The human rights dialogue between the European Union and China includes talks at the political level, academic discussions at the so-called expert level and cooperation projects between institutions and organizations.[1] China shares some traits with North Korea pertaining to the political system and security concerns voiced by the international community, despite some major differences between the two countries, especially with regard to size and political leverage. But lessons from China's human rights dialogue with the EU might be of use in the case of North Korea.

Dialogue Background, 1989–97

The fourth of June 1989 marks a turning point in China's relations with the outside world. The date carries a symbolic weight for non-Chinese scholars and activists as well as for the Chinese exile community. On that morning, the People's Liberation Army opened fire on unarmed protesters in the heart of Beijing and an unknown number of them were killed. Human rights in China had not been an issue at the international level until that

---

1. The basis for the different kinds of human rights dialogues in which the EU engages is formulated in the 'EU Guidelines on Human Rights Dialogues with Third Countries' of 2001.

day.[2] Opening up and market reform began in China in 1978 and the world market received the nation with open arms after 30 years of isolation, hoping to benefit from the fast-growing consumer market in the world's most populous country. But this incident in 1989 changed the picture. The Chinese leadership was heavily criticized and relations were severed in many different areas.

On 7 June, three days after the 'incident' (the official Chinese word for it), or the 'massacre' (the word used in most foreign media), the twelve European Union countries suspended economic and cultural relations with China, only gradually opening up again by the end of the following year.[3] Official visits were cancelled, development aid was discontinued, an arms embargo was adopted by the European Union and heavy criticism was voiced in UN settings. The Chinese leadership fought back with denials and claims of rights of national sovereignty and began to publish so-called 'white papers' on human rights, documenting progress in almost all areas. Contact was gradually re-established over the subsequent couple of years. At the same time, from 1990 and up through most of the new decade, the Western world, led by the United States and supported by the European Union, proposed resolutions to the Human Rights Commission condemning human rights violations in China.

At that time a resolution against a specific nation could be put forward by a single nation or a group of nations in the Human Rights Commission. Then other countries could put forward a so-called 'no-action motion', which had the effect that the resolution was not to be discussed and voted upon. If

2. Roberta Cohen (1987) 'People's Republic of China: The Human Rights Exception,' *Human Rights Quarterly*, vol. 9, no. 4, pp. 447–549.
3. David Gosset (2002) 'China and Europe: Toward a Meaningful Relationship,' *Perspectives*, vol. 3, no. 7.

the no-action motion received a majority of the votes, then the resolution fell and was not brought to a vote.[4] This procedure was certainly utilized liberally by the Chinese delegation in the wake of June fourth. From 1990 to 1997, eight resolutions were put forward criticizing China's human rights record. With only one exception, China succeeded each time in gathering so many votes for their no-action motion that the resolution was not discussed. But in 1995 China lost the motion; the resolution was voted upon and was almost adopted, with developing countries and China voting against and rich countries voting in favour.[5]

The Chinese government had anticipated this danger, and opened up for a human rights dialogue with the Europeans in the beginning of 1995,[6] presumably in order to prevent support for another resolution in 1996.[7] Two dialogue meetings were held, the first in January 1995 and the second in early 1996. But when the Chinese understood that the EU was going to vote for a resolution anyway, they broke off the process. This tug-of-war continued the following year and the Chinese made it clear behind closed doors that it was willing to resume the dialogue on the condition that the EU did not support a reso-

---

4. See www.unhchr.ch/html/menu2/2/rules.htm, rule 65, pt. 2. Accessed on 27 March, 2012.

5. E/CN.4/1995/L.86 in E/CN.4/1995/176: 388–391. In a dramatic move, Russia changed sides from one day to the next, first voting against China and then casting the decisive vote on China's side in the second round. Russia thus saved China the humiliation of having a resolution passed against them, and it is commonly believed that they were paid for this.

6. EU Commission (1995) 'Communication of the Commission: A Long-term Policy for China–Europe Relations.' COM (1995) 279/final. See http://eeas.europa.eu/china/docs/com95_279_en.pdf.

7. Robert Baker (2002) 'Human Rights, Europe and the People's Republic of China', *China Quarterly*, 169: 58.

lution.[8] At the same time, the unity of the European countries had gradually evaporated as memories of June fourth faded and several European countries were enticed by new, lucrative business deals in China.[9] The last attempt at getting a resolution adopted was made by Denmark in early 1997 but, with no united front, a UN resolution was a no-go and could even harm individual member countries economically so the exercise was not repeated. Other countries and regions took the same constructive-criticism path as the EU. Human rights dialogues with China were established with a host of other countries such as Australia, Brazil, Canada, Norway and Sweden.[10]

In Europe, invitations to a human rights dialogue meeting were sent out to member states in early 1998, and since that time the EU–China human rights dialogue has taken place regularly, with only a few interruptions caused by political tensions between the two parties. That the Chinese side had a strong wish to avoid resolutions was proven by its intensive lobbying for the no-action motion and, indeed, by its efforts to prevent the Commission's adoption of nation-specific resolutions at all, advocating that it should limit itself to thematic resolutions.[11] In 2011 researchers reported that China was still

8. Katrin Kinzelbach (forthcoming 2013) *The EU's Human Rights Dialogue with China. Quiet Diplomacy and its Limits.* London: Routledge.

9. Especially the sale of Airbus aircraft to China was at stake. This gave countries standing to gain financially from this, for example France and Germany, the derogatory nickname, the 'Airbus Club'.

10. Ann Kent (1999) *China, the United Nations, and Human Rights. The Limits of Compliance.* Philadelphia, University of Pennsylvania Press, p. 78; Caroline Fleay (2008) 'Engaging in Human Rights Diplomacy: The Australia–China Bilateral Dialogue Approach', *The International Journal of Human Rights*, vol. 12, no. 2, pp. 233–252; Sophia Woodman and Carole Samdup (2005) 'Canada's Bilateral Human Rights Dialogue with China: Considerations for a Policy Review'. Briefing paper, International Centre for Human Rights and Democratic Development, Montreal, Canada.

11. See the extensive study of Ann Kent (1999). Another example is discussed by Katrin Kinzelback in her empirical analysis, where she con-

investing much effort in avoiding resolutions against it in the Human Rights Council, and it consistently argues against the adoption of country-specific resolutions in all cases.[12] Again in March 2012, the Chinese delegation used a standard wording on the practice when explaining its opposition to a resolution criticizing North Korea and extending the Special Rapporteur mandate on that country:

> China was always in favor of appropriately resolving differences in human rights through dialogue and cooperation. China was against the use of resolutions for exerting pressure on certain countries. China expressed disappointment that members of the Council were continuing to target the Democratic People's Republic of Korea. Greater attention should be paid to difficulties faced in terms of economic, social and cultural rights in the country.[13]

The same expressions were used concerning a resolution on the human rights situation in Iran (see box), which was also adopted on the same occasion, at the 19th annual session of the Human Rights Council in Geneva.

North Korea likewise often protested against the whole idea of country mandates, as we have seen above. For example in 2009:

> The country-specific procedure which was a fundamental cause of the dissolution of the Commission on Human Rights continues to remain. There is no single country mandate on western countries. All such mandates are related to the developing countries. Therefore, the country mandates introduced

cludes that China in 2003 agreed to a visit by the Special Rapporteur on education, motivated by the fear of a critical resolution in the 2003 CHR session.

12. Author's notes from a roundtable in Chatham House, 30 November 2011.

13. See http://www.ohchr.org/EN/NewsEvents. Accessed on 27 March 2012.

The EU–Iran Dialogue on Human Rights

The history of the relations between Iran and the international community exhibits traits similar to the story of North Korea.

Iran was part of the club entitled the 'Axis of Evil' by George W. Bush in January 2002 together with Iraq and North Korea. Prior to that, Iran had been the subject of UN resolutions for almost twenty years from 1982-2002, and a Special Rapporteur had been assigned to the country since 1984. In spite of the Bush doctrine, the mandate of the Special Rapporteur was not prolonged in 2002, resolutions were discontinued and a dialogue with the EU was set up. The first meeting took place in December 2002.

In July 2002 the Iranian government sent out invitations to all the thematic rapporteurs, leading to plans for receiving the Special Rapporteur on women early in 2003. In December 2002 a moratorium on the practice of stoning was announced.[1] During 2003 to 2005, six Special Procedures visited Iran.[2]

---

1. DIIS Policy Brief, May 2011, *Dealing with Iran: How Can the EU Achieve its Strategic Objectives?*
2. Ineke Boerefin (2003) 'Human Rights Dialogues', *Netherlands Quarterly of Human Rights*, vol. 21, no. 1, pp. 3–6.

In June 2004 the EU issued a statement concluding that no progress in the human rights field had been made in Iran and, after much diplomatic maneuvering in the subsequent year, the resolutions were re-introduced, the dialogue stopped and resolutions against Iran in the UN system have been adopted every year since then.[3]

A policy brief from the Institute of International Studies in Copenhagen from May 2011 recommends that the EU defuse tensions with Iran by initiating discussions 'on non-controversial areas of mutual interest such as 'narcotics, trafficking ... energy policy, and improved response to humanitarian or environmental catastrophes'.[4]) The brief argues that the basic interests of the EU are better protected through exchange and cooperation with the Iranian government than through pressure and stigmatization on the international scene. The latter strategy only risks reinforcing hardliners in the Iranian government.

---

3. A/HRC/16/75: 45.
4. Seyyed Hossein Mousavian (2012) *Iran–Europe Relations. Challenges and Opportunities*. London: Routledge, pp. 216–217.

against the will of the countries concerned ... constitute a major source and institutional structure infringing upon the rights and interests of not only the DPRK but also the developing countries as a whole. The country-specific procedure should have been removed in conjunction with the dissolution of the Commission on Human Rights. (A/HRC/10/G/6: 4)

But the difference between China in 1997 and North Korea in the late 2000s is that China at that time was able to mobilize enough votes against a resolution among the other members of the Commission on Human Rights. Whether North Korea tried to do the same we cannot say, as its 'silent' diplomacy is not on record, but the North Korean delegation did complain, among other things, that the adoption of the first resolution in 2003 came as a surprise attack at the very last moment and that the countries behind it enforced its adoption through 'pressure and blackmail behind the screen.'[14] The wording gives the impression that North Korea might have tried to avoid the resolution by persuading other countries to vote against it, had they been 'warned' in due time. Anyway, it is probable that North Korea does not have enough friends in the world community to be able to mobilize enough votes and thus avoid this form of exposure.

The EU–China Dialogue Structure, 1997–2012

The EU–China human rights dialogue has since 1998 been running on three tracks:

- A political dialogue with participation of officials from China and the EU;
- Academic seminars, also called expert seminars;
- Bilateral or multilateral technical cooperation projects.

In theory, the three tracks should be mutually beneficial and be linked in time and substance. This has not always been the case. The intention of the parties to have meetings twice a year has not always been fulfilled; in 2003 due to the outbreak of SARS and in 2007 because of disagreement on the participation of international NGOs such as the China-critical organization, Human Rights in China, which is based in New York. Then in 2011, the bestowal of the Nobel Peace Prize on a Chinese prisoner caused the government to cancel political consultations. The political and academic meetings have often been placed close to each other in time, while the cooperation projects have lived their

---

14. A/HRC/5/G/11, p. 2.

own lives entirely, with only marginal relations to the other two levels. Each year two political sessions and two academic seminars have taken place, alternating between China and Europe. Political discussions have been held behind closed doors while information on the seminars is easier to find, though procedures for reporting or adoption of joint statements have not been consistent. A short description of topics and participants will follow below with greater weight given to the academic consultations, as most is known about them.

Each academic seminar typically has two themes, and these are grounded in both civil and social issues. Some of them are presumably also discussed at the political level. Such themes as the death penalty and torture have been discussed several times, but women's rights, the right to health and the right to education have also been on the agenda. Participants at the political level are officials, mostly from the ministries of foreign affairs but also from line ministries pertaining to the chosen topics. Participants in the seminars are mainly academics from Chinese and European universities and research institutions, but also staff from official circles like the Chinese Ministry of Foreign Affairs and the European Commission. On the European side, each member country selects its participants, but practices are not the same; some countries often send the same people, while other countries send new people each time. Some countries pick China scholars while others select researchers specialized in the topics to be discussed, and this means that many European participants know nothing about China. On the Chinese side, one think-tank close to the top of the political hierarchy, the Institute of Law under the Chinese Academy of Social Sciences, is in charge of the programme, and the coordinators there most often choose lawyers who are competent in Chinese law but know very little about Europe.

Dialogue – Challenges and Impact

The process of dialogue as it has developed in the way sketched above has its limits and challenges. The impact of it can be and has been discussed in stacks of books, articles and reports.[15] We will return to that at the end of this chapter. In general, one important issue worth considering is the compatibility between the objectives of the two sides in the 'cooperation'. Clearly, the two parties have different motivations for entering the dialogue. Bluntly speaking, the EU embarks on the journey with the aim of changing the Chinese system[16] while the Chinese are set on silencing the criticism of its human rights situation from the international community, and especially on avoiding the adoption of critical resolutions in the CHR, or, as it now is named, the Human Rights Council. The EU is partly influenced by outspoken actors like politicians and activists, who – perhaps with the noblest of intentions – demand a tough attitude on what is perceived as a brutal regime. China, on the other hand, seeks recognition as a responsible equal partner in international relations. Having two nearly contradictory aims does not seem conducive to a true dialogue, which, after all, means 'a conversation between two or more parties', if one consults a dictionary.[17]

15. See Fleay (2008); Woodman and Samdup (2005); and Jan Wouters (2007) *EU Human Rights Dialogues. Current Situation, Outstanding Issues and Resources*. Leuven Centre for Global Governance Studies, Policy Brief no. 1.

16. This aim is not clearly put in the guidelines from 2001, which are quite vague on the objectives. But participation in the process clearly supports the understanding expressed above. Similar views can be found in other material, e.g. a policy brief from 2007: 'The two aims of the HRD are to improve the human rights situation in the country with which the dialogue is initiated and to keep the channel of communication with regard to human rights open' Wouters (2007).

17. Wikipedia has this, among other things, to say about dialogue: 'Dialogue is not about judging, weighing, or making decisions, but about understanding and learning. Dialogue dispels stereotypes, builds trust, and

Concerning the academic seminars, the political nature of the whole exercise has turned out to be a major impediment to success. Neither China nor the EU is prepared to let academics discuss human rights freely with each other in such a relatively high-profile environment. As with North Korea, the Chinese leadership is very sensitive to being lectured. Actually, this goes for European leaders as well. The discussion of problems regarding human rights in Europe during the dialogue have not really been intended from the side of the EU and have, even in closed communications, been discouraged. From both sides, ministry or commission staff have participated in the academic seminars, thus giving it all a political twist – the two delegations do not mingle but keep apart during breaks and meals. This problem is reflected in several more or less internal or confidential evaluations or reports suggesting how to improve the seminar process. These include lamenting the overly rigid and technical presentation of legislation and the lack of knowledge and openness on both sides, as well as suggesting moving the seminars to academic institutions instead of hotels or separating financial support for academic cooperation from the political process. The vagueness of clearly defined objectives and benchmarks is also among the concerns expressed from all sides. Their conflicting goals preclude a common understanding of what it all leads up to. Related to that is a rather tense conflict on whether to end each session with joint statements. The Chinese have been rather strongly opposed to the publication of written agreements and the EU side has been just as eager to have some tangible results to show their constituencies back home.[18] The outcome has been that either

---

enables people to be open to perspectives that are very different from their own.'

18. The EU Commission is under pressure from international NGOs to make the process more transparent. FIDH and Human Rights

no statement has been made or two separate statements have been made in which each side reports its own understanding of what has been discussed.

The cooperative projects on the ground are less influenced by the political level and thus less exposed to political pressure, but they do not have very much leverage higher up in the system. The two problematic issues touched upon above – incommensurable goals and politicization – are not so strongly felt at the lowest level of the dialogue process, that is, in the implementation of cooperative projects. The project managers rarely participate at the higher levels, and although the projects always require approval from a higher political or academic level, the activities are not as exposed to political pressure; as a result, the atmosphere becomes less politicized. The project managers will actually often shy away from involvement in the other parts of the dialogue for fear of entering the politically sensitive stage.[19] On the other hand, the projects are often seen as being part of the dialogue and evaluations have stressed the positive contribution of cooperation on practical low-profile topics.[20]

in China, 2004, 'Preliminary Assessment of the EU–China Human Rights Dialogue'. Paper submitted to an EU–China HRD meeting: 15. On file with the authors.

19. Sophia Woodman (2004) 'Bilateral Aid to Improve Human Rights: Donors Need to Adopt a More Coherent and Thoughtful Strategy', *China Perspectives*, no. 51, p. 29.

20. See, for example, a review of the Swiss human rights dialogue with China. It is true that it is separated from the EU dialogue, but the discussions and concerns involved are very similar to what we see in the EU case. Thomas Richter and Frauke Seidensticker (2007) 'Evaluation of Switzerland's Human Rights Dialogue with the People's Republic of China'. Deutsches Institut für Menschenrechte, Berlin.

Has Human Rights Protection in China Been Improved?

Has the dialogue with China improved the protection of human rights in China? The question has been extensively debated, and naturally, many different positions have been put forward. In the present context, we have to discuss the issue if we want to argue for a dialogue type of process between North Korea and the Nordic countries or the international community. Basically, as could be expected, there are both strong positive and strong negative answers depending on the political position and the individual leanings of the observer. Overall, there is no doubt that human rights protection in China has improved over the last 30 years.[21] The rule of law has been strengthened compared to the late 1970s, when reforms began. The security of the individual, freedom of movement, freedom of association, access to justice and the like are more consolidated now than they were in Mao's era from 1949-1979. However, more progress has been made on the formal level than on the practical level, as much new legislation remains to be implemented. Black-letter law has to become law in practice. And a wide range of violations of fundamental rights continue to haunt part of the population. Still, a birds-eye view reveals a freer and more secure life for most Chinese citizens. Has the EU–China dialogue helped or halted this development? Technically it is impossible to measure, as there are no valid indicators to use, and it is possible to argue, as does Katrin Kinzelbach, that the 'EU–China human rights dialogue can be categorized as a policy failure.'[22] Her conclusion is the result

---

21. Randall Peerenboom (2007) *China Modernizes. Threat to the West or Model for the Rest?* Oxford: Oxford University Press.
22. Katrin Kinzelbach (forthcoming 2013) *The EU's Human Rights Dialogue with China. Quiet Diplomacy and Its Limits.* London: Routledge.

of an evaluation of the dialogue as a policy instrument, as she asks: 'Is the EU-China human rights dialogue a policy instrument that enables the EU to influence China's human rights policy and practice?' An answer will always depend on the nature of the question, and in the study she cannot document any direct links between the dialogue activities and domestic developments in China.

We pose a different question, one based on the simple conviction that richer countries have an obligation to help poorer countries and that it is impossible to help someone with whom you cannot communicate. Support for the people of North Korea presupposes recognition of their government in the form of extending an invitation to dialogue.

What Can Be Learned from the EU–China Dialogue?

The Chinese experience tells us that it is of utmost importance for an Asian country with a Confucian background to avoid public denigration, and leaders will be prepared to go a long way to avoid this. The moral implications of buying international influence by abstention from criticism may be debatable, but the fact is that this is how the international system works.

Now, one may ask whether discontinuing the adoption of critical resolutions on North Korea and dismantling the Special Rapporteur mandate will improve the lot of North Korean citizens, or whether the constructive dialogue with China since 1998 has produced better results than the confrontations in Geneva during the 1990s. We contend that the resolutions have not set a positive development in motion in North Korea, and that the human rights situation remains critical. Our visit to Pyongyang in the autumn of 2010 revealed a severe economic crisis and a desperate desire on the side of North Korean academics and officials to gain support and recognition. While the results of the EU–China dialogue are contested and the process has been far from flawless, one can hardly deny that China during the last decades has seen substantial improvements in its preservation of human rights. In comparison to the beginning of the reform period in the late 1970s, the rule of law is now stronger, personal security and freedom are greater and opportunities for public participation have expanded. The last decade has in general been characterized by a continued expansion in human rights maintenance, even though serious setbacks have been seen, especially since 2008. The overall situation is, however, far better now than in the 1980s.

The cases of China and North Korea are not fully comparable. Nonetheless, China and North Korea share important similarities in terms of political system; both are centres of attention in terms of international security concerns (albeit in different ways) and both have previously been singled out as especially grave violators of human rights. We therefore conclude that the China dialogue represents a good example of what is realistic and what is not when dealing with states that have authoritarian governments and a general allergy to international pressure. We will therefore put forth three preconditions for success based on the EU–China dialogue.

First, interaction requires a pragmatic approach on behalf of both parties, which means that the international community needs to alter its expectations as to how and where changes in human rights can be realized. Most importantly, interaction with the structure of power in a single-party system like North Korea has to accord with the priorities and commitments of the government in order to establish a basis for rational communication.

Second, communication on human rights protection needs to be low-key, concrete and practically oriented, and deal with non-sensitive issues, rather than be absolute and all-encompassing.[23] Communication on human rights protection could, for example, be differentiated so that instead of speaking of 'human rights violations', the international community could try discussing food supply, health care, renewable energy, clean water and/or primary education with the Pyongyang leadership.

Third, formally established dialogues like that between the EU and China are too easily dragged down into the quicksand of mistrust and mutual accusation. As we have seen, the EU-driven dialogues are meant to change the policies in the 'target country' – as the dialogue partner was referred to in one academic policy brief.[24] Most countries are not really interested in being lectured from the outside. At the level of academic seminars or technical cooperation projects, political tensions can be avoided and results more easily obtained.

What, then, do North Korean government officials actually think about such suggestions for dialogue? What obstacles do they perceive to greater openness, international assistance and cooperation? In the following chapter we will take a closer look at the situation as it appears to the North Korean officials in Pyongyang, based on our dialogue with them and our own observations.

---

23. The same argument was put forward in the conference 'Towards a Human Security Framework for North Korea. Promoting Human Rights through Pragmatic Approaches', in Chatham House, London, 2–3 December 2010.
24. Wouters (2007), p. 2.

Opposite: Children in a Pyongyang street

CHAPTER 4

A Visit to North Korea,
October 2010

We decided to visit North Korea in 2010 in order to discuss obstacles to and possibilities for co-operation in the human rights area. We found that there is an increasingly open mentality towards international cooperation among North Korean officials. However, from the North Korean perspective, the nuclear question and the trade embargo remain troublesome issues that are seen as political tools in a US agenda to isolate the country further. 'Human rights' in and of themselves are not seen as 'off the table' by North Korea. However, the perception among North Korean officials is that the concept 'human rights' is being politicized by the US to demonize North Korea worldwide. Thus, addressing 'human rights' as a general question will be difficult as long as US–North Korean relations remain problematic. This may not be a surprising finding. What may be surprising, however, is that despite these obstacles, we found that cooperation is both possible and meaningful in several areas that are indirectly linked to the North Korean capacity to sustain human rights. These are areas such as agriculture, health care and energy production where resources and know-how are badly needed. International cooperation projects are generally welcomed in such areas and would be a way to circumvent the general human rights stalemate and improve living conditions for the North Korean population.

Negotiations with the North Korean Embassy in Stockholm

The Nordic countries all have diplomatic relations with North Korea, and this has been the case since the mid-1970s. Up until the late 1980s, there were North Korean embassies in Stockholm, Copenhagen, Helsinki and Oslo. However, today only one embassy remains in the Nordic region, namely the one in Stockholm, and only Sweden has an embassy in Pyongyang.[1]

Traveling to North Korea is not impossible; there is a small but growing tourist industry and an infrastructure to accommodate foreign guests in the country. We did not go as tourists, though, and therefore we were required to discuss the purpose of our visit with North Korean diplomats in Stockholm and Beijing. At an earlier stage we had discussed the issue of human rights in North Korea with a high-ranking North Korean diplomat posted in Europe, and although this representative of the North Korean government was about to close the discussion before we even got started, he remained seated, stating only that he found this to be a very uncomfortable situation. However, after hours of 'soft diplomacy' from our side, he seemed to relax and at the end of the meeting he said that he could see and understand our point of view. But, as he said, 'This issue is very controversial, it will hardly be less controversial in my time, but hopefully my children will be able to discuss it without any problem.'[2]

---

1. The embassies were primarily closed due to North Korea's financial limitations.
2. Personal communication, Copenhagen, 2008.

Thus informed, we decided not to introduce the human rights issue head-on in our negotiations with the embassy, as we did not want our project to be stranded in a long and most likely troublesome dialogue with the embassy staff in Stockholm. Instead we introduced our project in a slightly different way, not entirely giving up the idea of getting close to our subject of interest. Thus, we stated our aim: as academics in the field of Asian studies, both of us are regularly approached by the media in the Nordic region. We wanted to go to North Korea to get a first-hand impression of the current situation in the country. This was accepted as a good reason, and we started to negotiate a programme that included talks with government officials, visits to different institutions and some trips outside of the capital.

In this way, we had an unproblematic dialogue with the Stockholm embassy, and through e-mail communication and some telephone calls, a programme was set up for our visit to Pyongyang. Our suggestions were basically accepted, and we accepted the few necessary changes requested by the North Koreans for the trip to be realized. We could not, however, get our visa from Stockholm, but would have to contact the North Korean Embassy in Beijing. We were assured that this was a simple formality, but since we had a plane from Beijing to Pyongyang the day after a Chinese holiday, and were supposed to pick up the visa the day we arrived in Beijing, we called the Stockholm embassy to check whether the staff at the embassy in Beijing was working that day. The answer was: of course they are, the holiday is Chinese, not Korean.

A Deserted North Korean Embassy in Beijing

A week later, we stood in front of closed gate of the huge North Korean embassy compound in Beijing. We rang the bell and waited. No answer. We rang again, longer this time. A voice then told us that the embassy was closed, but did not ask why we were ringing the bell. Walking all the way around the block, we found no gate open, no people to contact, and our plane was to leave at noon the next day. A very Korean-looking lady with an emblem on her chest came out, but she disappeared before we were able to address her. We thought more people might come out, so we decided to remain on the sidewalk in front of the embassy. After a while a car with diplomatic plates arrived. We approached the person inside, and he opened the window. When we informed him of our situation, he was a little puzzled: 'we always close the embassy on Chinese holidays', he said, 'they should have known that in Stockholm'. He was fortunately very kind and told us that even if he were unable to help us on the spot, if he could get our names he would prepare the papers and make sure that we were attended to as the first travellers to Pyongyang the day after. We arrived at 10 am and were out in a taxi 15 minutes later with our North Korean visas on our way to the Beijing airport. This flexibility and understanding from a North Korean diplomat was highly appreciated – a good omen, perhaps, for our coming visit?

The not entirely new Russian aircraft was nearly full of travellers flying to Pyongyang. The traditionally dressed stewardesses were kind and served a simple Korean meal. A screen showed pretty pictures from the country we were approaching, and soft Korean tunes filled the air. The flight was short and the quiet Kimcheak airport outside Pyongyang a nice alternative to bustling airports elsewhere. We were on the only plane arriving that day, and there were more than enough officials to welcome us and take care of the formalities. One of these formalities was the strange and, to us, paranoid rule of handing over our mobile phones, which were only to be picked up again on the way out of the country. Not that we actually needed them, but the formality still signalled a strictly controlled country. It was quite interesting to watch North Korean travellers coming home, as most of them carried huge quantities of boxes and packages besides the normal trunks and bags. As far as we could observe, they were not subject to any strict control. It seemed more as though the customs officers were helping them to get their belongings out to waiting cars, buses and trucks.

Arriving in Pyongyang

At the airport we were picked up by our official host, a well-dressed young man from the Ministry of Foreign Affairs with good language skills in German, English and Swedish. We decided to stick to English, as that was most comfortable for all three of us. The trip to our hotel brought us through the city. We were asked if we wanted to make a stop at the huge bronze statue of Kim Il Sung at the entrance to the city. This we politely declined, both to test whether we at all had a say in the programme and because this kind of courtesy call was strange to both of us. Our guide then made some calls from the car (yes, he used a mobile phone) and we wondered whether our refusal of his offer would negatively affect the level of our accommodations. Probably it did not, as we were offered nice rooms on the 20th floor of a hotel situated on a small island in the middle of the Taedong River with a good view over the city.

It would not be accurate to claim that the hotel was very busy, but there were quite a number of people around, and very many Koreans among them. Most of them looked like officials from different ministries, while some of them looked more like party officials from the countryside, not used to wearing suits and absolutely not used to places like this. And then there were a few Westerners, for instance a Swiss national representing

DHL, and arriving in a typical DHL car. We were not able to hide our surprise and asked him if DHL was already established in Pyongyang? Yes, why not, he responded. Well, not many Western companies are present, we said, and added: is there at all a basis for a DHL business in this city? At the moment they were not too busy, he retorted, but expectations were high that this would change, and then they would already be established. For us, the discovery that private foreign companies are operating in North Korea was a sign that North Korea is already willing to start relating to the outside world, so we started our meetings with the North Korean officials on a positive note.

Meeting with North Korean Representatives

The North Korean Ministry of Trade hosted our visit. During our stay we held talks with representatives from the Ministry of Foreign Affairs (MOFA), the Ministry of Health, the Ministry of Land and Environmental Protection as well as with the General Bureau for Cooperation with International Organizations (GBCIO).

Meeting with the staff of the different ministries in Pyongyang seldom reveals much else than the official line of the party and the government. Usually, the head of department or vice-minister basically sticks to his/her manuscript and follows a pre-decided position with no 'room' for the visitors to bring up issues. This is not much different from such meetings in other countries. However, in some cases such meetings can be more open and the agenda more flexible, and this is what we experienced in Pyongyang in 2010. During our meetings the general mood among the high-ranking officials was accommodating, and it seemed clear to us that they expected their country to open up and continue the reform process, although the word 'reform' was taboo in the politically correct vocabulary.

We observed a marked difference from the 1980s and early 1990s in expressed attitudes towards reforms. At an earlier visit in 2004 there was already a marked discrepancy between older and younger officials. The old guard still emphasized the difficult security situation while the younger generation revealed a more daring attitude and expressed a desire for their country to improve relations with the outside world. In this visit the generational discrepancy was less clear, as there was a general desire to establish international contacts and a readiness among the officials we met to admit local shortcomings and search for better solutions. Our impression was that it had become obvious to people working for the regime that the economic and technical problems were connected to the isolation of the country. Most people eagerly awaited the 'adjustments' (the official phrase) to the Juche ideology so that North Korea could benefit from knowledge and technical achievement in foreign countries.

North Korean Perspectives on Opening Up, Security and Human Rights

During our different talks, the sentiment of messages from the North Korean side was relatively uniform: a recurring statement was that North Korea urgently wanted to open its gates to the rest of the world; that the country needed a peaceful environment to be able to develop and get back to a sustainable economic and social situation; that the US created a hindrance to such a development; that the US played a destructive role that prevented rather than enabled dialogue; and that it was the US and not North Korea that was maintaining a Cold War mentality instead of pursuing cooperation, since the US continuously rejected the idea of entering into bilateral talks with the North. Moreover, North Korean officials maintained that the sustained economic sanctions and the continued pressure exerted by US joint military exercises with South Korea in waters neighbouring the Northern shores was seen as proof of their hostile intentions. Their view was that prospects for dialogue and interaction with the outside world were few as long as the rest of the world simply followed the US. Generally, this perception of the existence of a deliberate isolation strategy against North Korea is widespread among North Korean officials.

When discussing the human rights issue, the previous dialogue with the European Union was the vantage point. In 2001 the EU commission sent a delegation to Pyongyang, and North Korea agreed to enter a human rights dialogue with the European Union. Preparations were underway and a North Korean delegation was sent to Brussels in order to discuss cooperation in the field. However, in 2003 the EU decided to suggest what North Korean officials saw as an 'anti-DPRK' resolution in the UN Commission of Human Rights. Seen from the North Korean side this decision only emphasized the already existing perception among North Korean officials: that the human rights dialogue was subordinate to US policy and that the US stance on the nuclear question prohibited possibilities for cooperation in other areas. The nuclear weapons programme of North Korea was to be seen solely as a deterrent and therefore it was wrong of Western media to depict the leadership as a band of warmongers. Among the North Korean leadership there was a widespread conviction that the US and others were politicizing the human rights issue in order to demonize the country and muster support to prevent North Korea's nuclear development by imposing sanctions.

In general, these sanctions are of great concern to the North Korean officials. Not only do they reinforce the isolation of

North Korea but also they prevent development in the energy sector, which is a high priority area. North Korean government officials stressed that solving the energy problem by creating a sustainable energy supply consisting of both fossil fuels and re-newable energy technologies is one of the most pressing issues in North Korean politics. In the perspective of the leadership a stable supply of energy is simply the precondition for develop-ment and social progress, and the US-imposed embargo is a hindrance to the import of the necessary energy equipment.

Considerations on the Embargo

The trade embargo was addressed during all our meetings. Though it formally only targets 'nuclear-related, ballistic missile-related, or other weapons of mass destruction-related programmes',[3] it is clearly perceived as a major obstruction in almost all kinds of relations with the outside world. The embargo is on paper directed solely against military equipment and meant to prevent nuclear proliferation and it specifically excludes civilian goods with the wording 'except for humani-tarian and developmental purposes directly addressing the needs of the civilian population',[4] but it is apparently applied more broadly and is certainly perceived as being applied more broadly among North Korean officials and academics.

When reading through the two important UN Security Council resolutions on which the embargo is based (see box overleaf), one gets a picture of how they can be used to ban the entry and exit of an infinite number of products and to block cooperation on a wide range of activities. Since the wording in the resolutions is ambiguous, it leaves plenty of room for inter-pretation by the UN system as such, and even for individual

3.   S/RES/1718 (2009), 8(a)ii.
4.   Ibid., par. 19.

The North Korea Trade Embargo

The UN Security Council has imposed the trade embargo on North Korea in two stages.

The first step came when the UN Security Council adopted Resolution 1718 on 14 October 2006 as a reaction to the North Korean test of a nuclear weapon on 9 October of that year. For the first time the UNSC *determined* that 'there is a clear threat to international peace and security'.[1] The October resolution decided that North Korea *shall* abandon all nuclear weapons.

Sanctions were imposed in the form of a decision that all member states should prevent supply, sale or transfer as well as import of certain items to and from North Korea. The items are broadly related to the production of nuclear weapons and cover a myriad of different devices and products. However, 'luxury goods' are also on the list without any definition of what that might cover or any argument for why they are there. Resolution 1718 empowers member states to freeze the assets of persons or entities designated by the Security Council as being engaged in or otherwise supporting North Korean nuclear programs and it orders Member States to prevent entry or transit into their territories of these persons 'together with their family members'.[2]

The second step came in the summer of 2009, when Resolution 1874 was adopted as a reaction to a North Korean nuclear test of 25 May the same year. This resolution widens the embargo, among other things to include a ban on 'all arms and related material, as well as to financial transaction, technical training, advice, services or assistance related to the provision, manufacture, maintenance or use of such arms or material'.[3]

---

1. S/RES/1718.
2. S/RES/1718, par. 8e.
3. S/RES/1874, Par. 9.

member states. For example, states are called upon to 'exercise vigilance' regarding the supply, sale or transfer of small arms, to 'take the necessary steps' to prevent entry of certain persons into their territory, to inspect all cargo if it 'has reasonable grounds to believe' that the cargo contains forbidden items, or to take action 'in accordance with their national authorities and legislation', and so on. The gate is left wide open for any local authority to deny trade or exchange of services with North Korean goods and North Korean nationals. There is no mentioning in the resolutions of any mechanism for testing whether the sanctions imposed are actually necessary to prevent nuclear proliferation, nor is there an organ responsible for hearing complaints on the part of North Koreans whose survival has been threatened as a consequence of the embargo. Perhaps it is not surprising, then, to find that among the North Korean officials we met there is a good deal of scepticism with regard to the UN sanctions.

From the authors' point of view, the use of sanctions has not been successful in changing the attitude of the North Korean leadership. In addition, it has only worsened the human rights situation in the country. This is very much in line with what the respected human rights scholar, Katarina Tomasevski, concluded on a thorough study of donor human rights policies from 1997: 'The use of sanction challenges the essential principle of humanitarian law whereby civilians should not be purposefully harmed; in trying to punish 'a state' sanctions necessarily victimize its population and result in double victimization.'[5] The case of South Africa is often mentioned as the only success where sanctions are claimed to have contrib-

---

5. Katarina Tomasevski (1997) *Between Sanctions and Elections. Aid Donors and Their Human Rights Performance.* London and Washington: Pinter, p. 214.

uted to the elimination of apartheid. Even this claim cannot be sustained by solid evidence, and the special feature in South Africa was a strong and dynamic opposition movement that requested and made use of the sanctions. This feature is totally absent in the case of North Korea.

North Korean Perspectives on Human Rights

While the embargo was surely an important factor in the minds of the North Koreans we met, the main reason for the embargo (the nuclear issue) was only briefly touched upon. The same can be said for the other clear impediment to the desired exchange and interaction with the outside world: the human rights question.

Global security and human rights have been the two red lights obstructing 'normal' communication between North Korea and the rest of the world since the beginning of this century. A threat to global security emanating from North Korea is captured in the prism of the nuclear issue, while sustenance of human rights (or human security, as some prefer to call it[6]) in North Korea immediately brings pictures of mass starvation and labour camps to the minds of many people in the West. As was anticipated, the human rights situation in the country was not addressed directly by the people we talked to, and there was no direct reference to the battle over the 'resolutions' in the UN Human Rights Council. It is quite likely that the North Korean representatives had been instructed not to talk about these issues, or perhaps they did not have enough detailed knowledge of them. However, in light of the great importance that North Korea officially attaches to the UN resolutions, it is

---

6. Chatham house conference programme, 'Towards a Human Security Framework for North Korea: Promoting Human Rights through Pragmatic Approaches', 2–3 December 2010.

worth noticing that they did not 'play the UN card', that is, they did not deliberately present themselves as 'victims' of unjust persecution by the whole world. The topic of human rights was addressed only on our initiative.

Sectors Lacking Resources, but Open to Cooperation

Despite the reluctance to discuss human rights head on, the North Korean representatives addressed several issues and needs that are directly or indirectly linked to the capacity to sustain human rights: the capacity to improve living conditions for the population. Most important among the issues highlighted by the officials were problems and shortcomings in the agricultural sector, the public health sector and the energy sector. Providing food and general supplies, medical and technical equipment, energy to support the irrigation systems and, not least, expertise, were mentioned as basic needs. A very serious problem acknowledged by several of the people we met, although they had no suggested solution to it, was the non-existent links between sectors and institutions located in different regions or belonging to different governmental departments or offices. This horizontal mode of organizing the economy seems detrimental to the creation of effective means of production. Farms located relatively near to each other, albeit in different administrative zones, apparently had no practice of assisting each other in solving problems related to production – or if they did want to attempt this, it had to go through a central body. As politics in North Korea is a top-down activity, we understood that inquiries from the periphery to the centre were cumbersome, time-consuming, perhaps even unheard of. One indication of the gravity of the situation was that we were asked whether *we* could provide probiotic bacteria for producing yoghurt. It is difficult to understand that the natural environment should not possess bacteria that could be used for souring milk. And strange, as well, that the managers of the cooperative we visited seemed to find it easier to ask foreign visitors than neighbouring colleagues.

Two examples of the great needs challenging the agricultural sector were revealed when we visited some animal farms outside Pyongyang. The first was a dairy-producing farm with cows descending from stock imported from Germany back in 1964. Obviously, they were now inbred and made a pitiful impression. Neither milk nor meat could be expected in larger quantities – the remedy would be semen from other stock. It was heart-breaking to observe skilled farmers with no remedy for this sorry state of affairs. Another visit to a goat farm revealed a new problem. The buildings were adequate and the dairy facilities to produce yoghurt, milk and cheese were present. Consistency and taste were excellent, but the truck from Pyongyang often failed to arrive on time. Technical problems, a flat tire, no diesel fuel, many reasons were behind this, but the result was that a large part of this good food was wasted, and the people in the city had to do without it. We asked why they did not have their own means of transportation. We were told that it was a kind of division of labour, obviously not a problem that was left to people on the ground to solve. In both cases, the North Koreans were quite open about their problems, which underscored clearly that we had not been taken to model institutions. That we visited these places could thus be interpreted as a cry for help and assistance.

Our meeting with the public health sector did not reflect the same attitude as to the need for outside help. We met with the staff of a local health clinic in a Pyongyang suburb at which the chief physician was simply too proud to admit to any shortcomings. Our questions were not taken at face value, but as implicit criticisms of the political system, and not dealt with kindly. Compared with visits to such facilities in earlier field trips, it was quite clear, however, that medicine and utensils were scarce, heating a luxury permitted only in one room, and electricity an unsteady commodity. All this greatly affected the work done at the clinic. Instead of discussing this difficult situation, the proud and politically loyal chief of the clinic talked about all the many victories of the revolution. Asked what kind of support they might need from the outside world, she replied that they would be interested in technology to ease the pain of women in labour. Her staff seemed uncomfortable with the situation and would probably have told another story, if permitted. Our guide excused the chief physician, saying that she had once headed a well-functioning clinic but that times were now difficult.

In the energy sector, the lack of power was stressed time and again by representatives from different ministries, not least since this obstructed the functioning of large parts of the irrigation system. The energy shortages thus spilled over into the agricultural sector. North Korea once used to receive delegations from less-developed countries in Asia, Africa and Latin America who came to inspect and learn from the nation's well-developed irrigation system. One construction site linked to this system is the Nampo barrage, a dam on the west coast which has made it possible to reclaim land and regulate the freshwater reservoirs fundamental to irrigation, as well as making it possible for ships to enter the Taedong river system through a system of lock-chambers in the dam. This construction site is still the pride of the system, a place to which foreign guests are taken. We also visited this site, and although our local guide assured us that everything worked well, the fact is that the overall irrigation system hardly works due to lack of a stable energy supply. This has extremely negative implications for food production and thus the welfare and health of the population. However, what should be noted here is that these huge irrigation systems and all the construction work that is necessary for them to function – building and maintaining dams, water reservoirs, channels and pumping stations – testify that the government indeed has a strategy for enhancing food production. This should be borne in mind when the North Korean authorities are accused of totally neglecting their impoverished population.

Could Agriculture, Health and Energy Represent Areas for Cooperation?

As is illustrated by the above examples, the agricultural, public health and energy sectors undoubtedly lacked the necessary resources to function. Moreover, the North Koreans welcomed international cooperation in these specific areas. Officials from the Ministry of Land and Environment Protection and the Ministry of Agriculture expressed great interest in agricultural cooperation, for example in the form of cooperative projects on biological pest control, development of biomass and organic farming procedures. In the energy sector, there was great interest in possibilities for carbon trade, which is not affected by the current embargo. The issue of clean development mechanisms (CDMs), a concept highlighted in the Kyoto Protocol, was mentioned several times as an area of great interest in which both North Korean scholars and administrators need further knowledge and guidance. Interest in cooperation on sustainable energy production, such as wind energy, was also expressed. In other sectors, business law and emergency risk management were mentioned as potential areas for cooperation and exchange of information.

From the human rights perspective, cooperation with North Korea in areas such as food security, health care and energy could greatly benefit the living conditions for the North Korean population. Obviously, one needs to clarify which projects are possible and which are not under the current UN embargo. It certainly is hard to see how cooperation projects in these areas could strengthen North Korea's military capabilities (the reason often highlighted as an argument for prohibiting such projects) – food supplies, medical equipment and wind turbines are hardly essential to building nuclear bombs. Thus, cooperation in the above-mentioned areas seems both plausible and constructive. It would be a way to circumvent the human rights stalemate caused by the problematic relations between North Korea and the US and its allies, and help alleviate the grave living conditions of the North Korean population.

A few points from the case of the EU–China human rights dialogue should be reiterated here. Although the level of political dialogue has thus far not yielded significant results, it has enabled the facilitation of academic seminars and technical cooperation projects. Since the technical cooperation projects have been allowed to function more or less independently, they have avoided entanglement in the highly politicized atmosphere of the political dialogue. Thus, it is at the level of technical cooperation project that tangible results have been achieved. The same structure and facilitation might be expected in the North Korean case, although the North Korean leadership is known to be even more allergic to political criticism than the Chinese leadership. A lesson from the dialogue between the EU and China of relevance for a future dialogue with North Korea is that it is important to strike the right balance between cooperation and criticism at the level of political dialogue. Otherwise one risks jeopardizing those academic seminars and technical cooperation projects that are already in place and that could have a potential positive effect on the welfare of the population.

Who Should Steer an Initiative of this Type?

Given the European Union's mixed experiences with engaging in human rights dialogue with North Korea, it may be wise to have another entity initiating a new dialogue. The Nordic countries could join forces and approach North Korea for an interchange on how to promote concrete joint projects targeting the above-mentioned areas. Three things point to why the Nordic countries stand out as the obvious candidates for this.

First, all five Nordic countries have long-standing diplomatic relations with North Korea (since the mid-1970s) and have experience in dealing with the regime via diplomatic channels, not least through active Swedish diplomacy and a long-standing presence as active participants in international NGO activities. Second, from the perspective of the North Korean government, the Nordic countries are not seen to be involved in US efforts to limit, isolate and change the regime. Thus, the Nordic countries are considered to be relatively neutral to North Korean interests – an important condition when dealing with a sometimes paranoid regime.

Third, *the social-democratic character* of the Nordic welfare societies (irrespective the political colour of their government) represents a common ground for dialogue and cooperation. It may be easier for North Korean officials to enter into dialogue with delegations from countries that have societal characteristics that are recognizable to them, for instance, a great degree of government intervention in the economy, a strong tradition for redistribution of income, and publicly run education and health care systems.

Building the capacity of human capital is a very important aspect of cooperation with North Korea. The Nordic countries are relatively strong on renewable energy, public health and education, areas that are specifically important for peaceful North Korean development. Currently, there are too few North Korean scholars present at international conferences and meetings in the above-mentioned fields. This is something the Nordic countries can help to change. To help academics to catch up in their different fields of study, invitations could be issued through Nordic institutions with expertise in fields where North Korea lags behind.

CHAPTER 5

Conclusions and Perspectives

*T*he aim of this book is to improve our understanding of North Korea, its relationship to the international community, and the bureaucrats populating its political system, and to draw on concrete experiences to give some suggestions as to how a human rights dialogue could be established. North Korea has been engaged in the international human rights regime since the early 1980s, but up until now, its interactions with the UN human rights system have not been successful in improving the situation of human rights in the country or in creating an environment for continued dialogue and cooperation. Efforts to invite the cooperation of North Korea on specific areas of human rights have been particularly difficult, since the country has simultaneously been singled out as a gross violator through the adoption of UN resolutions. Based on analyses and arguments presented in this study, we contend that creating a constructive dialogue and establishing cooperation with North Korea in the area of human rights is a possibility. However, certain aspects of North Korea's current relations with the world around them should be taken into account.

The Necessity of Building Mutual Trust

Since fear and distrust are the two strongest emotions characterizing relations between North Koreans and the international community, it is obviously easier said than done to achieve positive change. A first step, however, is increased contact between North Korea and the rest of the world. As this is written, the American Press Agency (AP) has decided to establish a permanent office in Pyongyang with a staff of two. The office will be located in the same building as the North Korean National Press. Some observers see this as a naïve move pointing out that, if AP believes that its staff will be able to report freely from North Korea, they probably also believe in Santa Claus. Another interpretation is that the American agency is prepared to invest in an effort to build trust – and probably even a professional relationship. If the two AP representatives are ready to report on issues other than the 'usual suspects' (the nuclear issue, human rights violations) they might help to broaden our understanding of North Korea. Moreover, they might influence their local counterparts to add a bit of spice to the rather boring North Korean news outlets; this would be a desirable first step in a new direction for the North Korean state media. If, however, their task is to find proof for what we already suspect is happening behind the closed doors and fences of the North, their stay will probably be a rather short one.

It is by no means an easy task to open up a country afflicted with double isolation: internally due to Juche (and as long as this ideology has any meaning, 'opening up' will be seen as a hostile word) and externally due to an ongoing trade embargo and the general animosity expressed by foreign countries. But there are ways and means, and there are experiences indicating that increased contact mostly has a positive effect on the relationship. If personal relations can be positively affected by increased contact, then more general relations between institutions and national representatives can be, too. During the long period of on-and-off meetings in the six-party group, representatives of the two main adversaries, North Korea and the US, developed a certain understanding of each other's positions and, according to sources close to the two leading diplomats, a certain affinity on the more personal level.[1] This happened to such an extent that the conservative media in Japan nick-named the American chief negotiator at the time Chris 'Jong' Hill (Christopher Hill), indicating that he might be going too 'soft' on the North Koreans due to this special relationship. An American head of the Kedo light-water reactor project, staying in North Korea for about a year, later published a book, *Living With the Enemy*, which provides vivid examples of how time and continued contact positively affected the relations between him and the people with whom he was working.[2] On his way out of the country, the author describes a situation that easily could have created problems: lining up for the customs control at the local port, he realized that the boxes he had packed was too big to pass through the screening machine. When the customs chief then asked about the content of the boxes, the outgoing head of the Kedo project said: 'books and clothes.' He recounted, 'After a short pause, the chief looked me directly in the eye and calmly said, "That's ok, Representative Saccone, I trust you." His expression struck straight to my heart. I never expected to hear those words from a North Korean to an American. In one sense I could not have asked for a finer conclusion to my tour of duty.'[3] This American found that a rather cold and suspicious attitude towards each other at the start developed into an interpersonal understand-

1. Personal communication, Seoul 2006; New York 2006; Como, Italy, 2008.
2. Saccone, Richard, 2006, Living with the Enemy: Inside North Korea. Seoul: Hollym International Corp.
3. Ibid., pp. 318–319.

ing, and after a while trust was built – which greatly helped to solve even complex problems in the relationship.

As only few people have ever visited North Korea, and even fewer have stayed there for long periods, another way of establishing contact and contributing to assisting North Korea towards reform would be to invite people out of the country. Such visits are possible, although rare. But they take place, and the journey functions as an educational experience. Although we cannot know how the visitor interprets what he or she sees and experiences, it is quite clear that what they see is different from what they know back home. At least, the visit functions as proof that methods different from those back home exist, and they can probably see that some alternatives to Juche do work quite well.[4]

Observers often point to the military expenditures of an impoverished North Korea as a main obstacle to improving the country's international relations and thus to development and growth. Such analyses are solely focused on the current situation, and neglect the historical causes and contexts. Briefly stated, the problem is not North Korea's strength but its weakness. Realistically, therefore, human rights in North Korea must be linked with the security of the regime.[5] It has to extend to the elite as well, including the political leadership. A simple first step would be for the US to recognize Pyongyang and establish an embassy in the capital, as several European countries already have done. A real dialogue on human rights

---

4. NIAS initiated and organized a North Korean–Nordic meeting in Shanghai in 2005, and a visit by a North Korean sustainable energy delegation to the Nordic countries in 2008. The foreign ministries of Denmark, Norway and Sweden sponsored these activities.

5. North Korea is weak in comparison to South Korea and the US, and feels threatened by these stronger nations and their allies. Thus, they allocate much of their scarce resources to the military, which is highly problematic from a humanitarian perspective.

with North Korea would definitely gain from a normalization of relations between North Korea and the rest of the world, in particular the US. As long as North Korea is recognized as an independent nation by most European countries and in the UN, their legitimate national interests must be recognized. Therefore, the government in Pyongyang should be dealt with as a relevant partner in international affairs, not as a pariah state nor as an honorary member of the '*Axis of Evil*'.

How the Human Rights Question Might Be Approached

In a recent conference dealing with the human rights situation in North Korea it was stressed that the way South Korea was described in the 1960s and 1970s in Western media (for example, in the *New York Times*) resembles descriptions of North Korea today. However, in that period, Western governments – and in particular the Korean-American minority in the US – did not care much about the human rights situation in the South. This same group is currently highly alarmed by the human rights situation in North Korea, which demonstrates that their concerns are, in part, politically motivated. Other groups in the US have similar political motivations, for example, 'Christian rights fundamentalists and naïve college students who are selective in their choice of information' as one American participant at the conference phrased it.[6] From the perspective of government offices in Pyongyang, 'human rights' and 'change of regime' have become synonymous, and unfortunately this has not only discredited those who misuse a good cause but all foreigners engaged in the human rights situation in North Korea. This is regrettable but, just like so many other difficulties in the incipient dialogue between North Korea and the outside world, it is a given condition. Distrust is widespread

---

6.   Personal communication, London, 2010

where trust is needed. Any attempt to place the blame for this unfortunate situation on either side is counter-productive, and it would hardly be possible to reach an agreement on this issue. The Western concept of human rights is somewhat foreign to East Asia in general. Thus, in a country where most people are lacking the basics needed for daily life, and indeed, in many cases, for survival, it might be better to approach the issue from another angle. 'Rights' might sound confrontational in an East Asian context, so why not talk about 'human dignity and security'? In humanitarian efforts to secure human survival and preserve human dignity, work with agriculture, the environment, water supply, sanitation, reforestation and electricity become relevant.

Because the 'change the regime' approach has completely failed – not only in its efforts to achieve change but also in efforts to improve living conditions for the North Korean people – we argue that establishing relations with the regime is more efficient. In more than one sense, the regime has an interest in providing for and helping its population. A main issue for any government with an ambition to stay in power is securing the survival of the population, seeing to it that babies and young children receive sufficient food so they remain healthy, and ensuring that the people is able to perform basic tasks and functions. Every economic and material need that is secured underpins the development of other positive changes in a society hungry for improvements and a better life. So far, the role of the ordinary citizens of North Korea has been misunderstood and underestimated. The North Korean people are not indifferent to politics but, as long as an almost chronic economic crisis hinders normal life, their main interest is in sustaining their livelihood and improving the conditions of daily life. Currently, what drives people in North Korea more than ideological guidelines is the struggle for survival. They are highly affected by ideology and disciplined by the political system, but they are not robots. An improvement in living conditions for the people of North Korea may enable them to participate more in the society and thus to achieve gradual change.

If 'human dignity' and 'human security' are introduced as issues on which North Korean government agencies could work with external agents – state-run, NGO and private enterprise – it is quite likely that the confrontations characterizing the 'human rights' agenda could be avoided. In that case, doors might be opened, or at least not kept completely shut. Human dignity and security could be turned into a matter for practical, positive discussion focusing on how both internal and external forces best could cooperate to reach results. The discussion could then also include broader issues, such as initiatives to combine human security with sustainable development. This book, then, arrives at four conclusions, which are given below.

Conclusions

First, we need a better understanding of North Korea's decision-making process in international politics. North Korea's compliance/non-compliance with the human rights regime is part of a larger geopolitical picture within which the actions of the world outside have a great effect on North Korean behaviour. When consulting historical experience, it is evident that a stronger North Korean commitment to the UN system of human rights ran parallel to Kim Dae Jung's Sunshine Policy (1998–2007), the more positive and constructive US approach during the Clinton administration (as attested to by the successful visit made by Secretary of State Albright in October 2000), and the EU-initiated human rights dialogue in 2001. However, from 2002 and onwards, North Korean commitment to cooperation in the UN system deteriorated. This change in North Korean behaviour correlated with US president George W. Bush's condemnation of the country as part of the 'Axis of Evil', the adoption of the US National Security Strategy in September 2002, and the European Union's initiative to sponsor the afore-mentioned UN resolution in 2003. Such drastic changes in the outside world's approach were reflected in North Korea's com-mitment (or lack thereof) to the human rights regime as, from then on, the channels of communications were obstructed. Any discussion on human rights with North Korea ended *de facto* with the resolution of April 2003.

Second, 'human rights' should be approached pragmatically by separating sensitive and non-sensitive issues and dealing with them accordingly. Due to the strong influence of East Asian political culture and its specific political organization, the North Korean regime is extremely allergic to political criticism from the outside.[7] Thus, successful interaction with a single party system such as the North Korean requires that one take into account the priorities and commitments of the govern-ment in order to set up grounds for constructive communica-tion. So far, treating 'human rights' as an all-or-nothing issue has not improved the human rights situation in the country. Instead, both sides have all too easily politicized any dialogue,

---

7. The political and ideological system of North Korea is 'totalitarian' according to the textbook definition. This implies everything which denotes the opposite of good government – evil comes to mind as well. Whether our textbook definition should be ascribed universal validity is still a matter of discussion. However, viewed in the light of traditional East Asian political culture, North Korea might not stand out as an ideal model, but neither would it be the ultimate illustration of the worst thinkable system. National pride, patriarchal authority and hierarchical institutions, not to mention historical wounds and animosities, affect politics and political relations throughout East Asia, and thus are relevant facets in the total picture of the North Korean system. This should be taken into account when approaching regime representatives allergic to political criticism from the outside.

leading to a disruption of communication. Instead, a pragmatic approach should be adopted. Such an approach could possibly lead to concrete and low-key cooperation projects in areas such as agriculture, health care, and renewable energy and thus improve basic living conditions for the North Korean population at large.

Third, other cases show that cooperation and dialogue on human rights with authoritarian regimes is often both feasible and more effective than confrontation and isolation. Although China's case is not fully comparable to that of North Korea, the two share important similarities in terms of political system and previous experiences within the international human rights regime. The EU–China dialogue is far from exemplary, but it represents a good example of what could be expected when dealing with states that have authoritarian governments and a general allergy to international pressure. The three-tier structure of the China dialogue has its strengths at the second (academic seminars) and third (technical cooperation projects) levels. Here, political tensions are more easily avoided and results more tangible. Therefore, in the case of North Korea, dialogue at the first level (political level) should not be expected to provide results but to serve as a means to facilitate cooperation on the second and third levels, at which communication and projects for the protection of human rights could be allowed to take on a more practical, low-key and concrete form.

Fourth, the establishment of concrete cooperative projects could improve living conditions for the North Korean population – and thus human rights. Our visit to North Korea in October 2010 and subsequent research make it clear that in the West currently there is a lack of both knowledge and understanding of the variety of perceptions and expectations to be found within the North Korean elite when it comes to communication with the world outside and an understanding of the human rights issue. North Korean officials in general reflect a considerable willingness to cooperate with international partners and to seek better relations with the outside world. However, the nuclear question and the trade embargo remain problematic issues seen as political tools in a broader US-initiated isolation strategy. 'Human rights' have also, in the eyes of North Korean officials, been politicized by the US in order to demonize the country as part of this same strategy. Despite these obstacles, cooperation is both welcomed and feasible in areas that are indirectly linked to North Korea's capacity to improve living conditions for its people. In these areas, know-how and resources are badly needed to alleviate the grave situation of the population. Moreover, cooperation projects in these areas would hardly strengthen North Korean military capabilities; sustainable food production, a functioning health care system, and wind or water turbines are hardly essential to building nuclear bombs or chemical weaponry. Cooperation in these areas could possibly circumvent the current human rights stalemate.

EPILOGUE

From Unresolved Stalemate towards Sustainable Development and Change

The current head figure in Pyongyang, Kim Jong Un, is a third-generation dictator in a regime that was seen as doomed to collapse when his grandfather died in 1994. To continue waiting for regime collapse in North Korea is not only unrealistic; from a humanistic point of view it is also irresponsible. This is what we have sought to convey with this book, which could be seen as 'a user's manual' to North Korea. In this short epilogue, in condensed form we shall suggest a way out of the long overdue stalemate because the present situation is harmful for all parties with stakes in the conflict, and first and foremost harmful to the North Korean population.

Why has the leadership in North Korea resisted change for so long? Isolation, self-made as well as imposed, is part of the answer. A long and very strong tradition with a patriarchal and hierarchical social fabric, which interacts with and guides the formation and realization of authority, is another. Then come the division of the country, an all-encompassing war and, in its aftermath, the establishment of two competing regimes, each of whom has used the other to preserve its own authority and power. South Korea's dictatorship operated within the framework of the free world as a line of defence against communist dictatorship – albeit with many traits similar to those of the enemy. Democratic transition came in South Korea as a result of popular struggle involving religious forces, students, workers and leading intellectuals, but also as a result of external pressure from international allies and partners. This pressure was both a push and a pull: authoritarian political practices were criticized but more important and effective was the influence from Koreans who came back after having studied abroad, most of them in the USA.

In comparison, North Korea's dictatorship has benefited from isolation, making self-sufficiency their all-encompassing state ideology and keeping foes as well as friends at a distance. The recent UN-sanctioned tightening of the embargo against North Korea due to its nuclear and missile tests, no matter the intention of this punishment, basically only assists the forces within the regime that reject an opening to the world, thus preserving its isolated status and preventing change from affecting North Korean society and its political regime.[1]

How, then, to start a process of change in an area suffering double isolation, self-imposed as well as externally supported? It goes without saying that a precondition is to end this isolation and promote the establishment of relations that make possible the positive impacts of external forces. From a human relations perspective, this is widely accepted common sense. It is also

---

1. Donald Gregg, former head of CIA in South Korea (1973–76), security advisor to G.H.W. Bush in the 1980s and US Ambassador to Seoul (1989–99), recently stated that 'The sanctions were a very foolish reaction to the North Korean rocket launch and should never have been imposed, given the knowledge that the South Korean government was behind them.' (The Hankyoreh, http:English.hani.co.kr/popups/print.hani?ksn=568744) download date: 10.02.2013.

supported by numerous studies within the social sciences showing that people react positively to positive approaches and negatively to negative ones. Expectations held prior to actual inter-personal contacts colour and may strengthen actions and reactions in a positive or negative direction accordingly. As international relations are conducted by people, prior expectations also affect such relations. Relations with North Korea are no exception. Positive relations beget trust, negative relations beget distrust. On a scale from zero to ten on trust between parties, the level characterizing relations between North Korea and the rest of the world is zero – both ways.

A condition for anything positive to come out of a relationship initially characterized by mutual distrust is to accept that the given conditions are simply the only possible point of departure. In relation to North Korea, this means that the present authorities must be acknowledged as those with whom one has to negotiate. Between parties where trust is lacking, formal, mutual respect has to be the point of departure. There can be no exception for international affairs. Regardless of differences in basic values, norms, ideological outlooks and political opinions, the expressed concerns of both sides must be taken seriously.

Engaging in talks in the absence of mutual trust on issues where the parties concerned are positioned at opposite poles from the outset demands discipline and strong goal-orientation: the final goal must give the process, the line of activities, its direction. Based on experiences discussed in the previous chapters, the human rights issue must therefore be approached pragmatically, using areas in which the parties have overlapping interests as well as practical abilities as the point of departure in order to reach something both sides consider a positive result.

In the present situation, positive results can be anything and everything that helps maintaining peace in the region and makes life better for the North Korean people. In a society marked by scarcities of food, energy, heating, transportation, health care and almost every other necessity of a well-functioning societal life, it seems insensitive to focus on political rights as a first priority, even if this can be defended philosophically as a prerequisite for a long-term, sustainable solution.

North Korea needs development assistance, but this is not on the priority list of Western – or Eastern – donors at the time of this writing. What have been realized in North Korea hitherto are a few, geographically scattered, small-scale projects based more on what donors were able to offer than on local needs. An improvement would be to develop institutional co-ordination of existing, planned and future projects, obviously together with North Korean representatives and preferably together with an international organization with a permanent presence in North Korea. The International Red Cross and Red Crescent Movement comes to mind as a relevant partner. It seems obvious that the positive effects of moderate input to a country in great need could be maximized by a much-needed coordination.

A coordinating office would at this stage be a useful instrument to bridge the gap between local needs and the diverse contributions of international donors, and thus an effort to maximize the impact of the assistance given.

The immediate and urgent needs of the North Korean population that the international community must address from a human rights perspective are, first, continued and increased provision of food and medical aid; thereafter, preconditions for the reestablishment of local food production and preservation must be supported. Related to this urgent task is the need to assist in developing the energy sector. This is a gigantic endeavour requiring long-term coordinated international assistance.

Currently, lesser but still substantial efforts can bring about the refurbishing of existing hydropower plants, old as well as relatively new ones, and the development of new, sustainable de-centralized power plants linked to concrete projects such as village development, establishment of health clinics, food processing factories and other types of production units.

In addition to project assistance, updated knowledge on technical matters related to the projects and their economic and technical management and maintenance is needed. Furthermore, related to international aid and assistance, knowledge of inter-cultural communication is called for. This need is something both parties – providers as well as receivers – have in common. Such educational efforts are desirable, something that is acknowledged by the authorities in Pyongyang, but the issue is also highly controversial and is seen by them as potentially dangerous to the survival of their authority and thus of the regime itself. It is in this contested field where attention to the needs can translate into threats that serious development assistance can change life conditions for people affected by these activities. In the longer run it can possibly affect the way that people – leaders and followers alike – organize their society.

This is essential: *for leaders and followers alike.* A commonly held, but probably incorrect, assumption in our part of the world is that inefficient regimes and their incompetent or bad leaders are doomed to remain as they are – unchangeable enemies to be defeated. This dualistic view of good and bad can hardly be sustained by real-life experience. A more reasonable view based on recent experiences of the processes of change in former dictatorships around the world would be that leaders and their aides – as well as the people – are adjusting, more or less smoothly, more or less willingly, to the actual circumstances in the world within which they function. The post-Cold War period can be seen as a global laboratory for economic, political and societal transformation. Changes in circumstances produce changes in people, and leaders are no exception.

The directions of these changes is not uniform as there are different roads to modernization, different answers to the challenges of our times. The path ahead for North Korea depends on, among others, the given political culture in the country and in the region that has formed and guided people in the past as it still does at present, although now combined with fresh ideas, impressions and influences from the outside world. It seems timely to encourage the governments in the West to do their part – it is not enough simply to wait for miracles to happen in Pyongyang. The formula is quite simple: achievement of a positive result requires positive interaction; the more positive interaction with North Korea, the greater the chance of a positive and sustainable result.

A great contribution could come from the Nordic region of Europe, where the five countries – Denmark, Finland, Iceland, Norway and Sweden – have institutionalized mutual consultations and cooperation, and have created a sense of community among people in a region formerly tormented by animosities, conflicting relationship and war. Assistance from the Nordics would be welcomed in North Korea and thus increase the possibilities of a positive impact of this relationship.

Timeline for North Korea and Its International Relations Pertaining to Human Rights

Mid-1980s and early 1990s
Two attempts at economic reform in North Korea.

11 May 1993
UN Security Council calls on North Korea to reconsider its decision to withdraw from the Nuclear Non-Proliferation Treaty.

11 June 1993
US–North Korea Joint Statement.

1994
Death of Kim Il Sung.
First nuclear crisis.

Summer 1998
Kim Jong-il indicates he is open to change on economic policy.

May 2000
Kim Jong-il's first public trip to China.

15 June 2000
Pyongyang Declaration.
Inter-Korean summit. Agreement on working towards re-unification in the form of a federation/confederation (signed by Kim Dae-jung and Kim Jong-il).

Exchange visits of separated families on one occasion. Economic cooperation.

October 2000

US–North Korea joint communiqué. Madeleine Albright visits Pyongyang (positive outcome).

January 2001

Kim Jong-il visits China again.

June 2001

Human rights dialogue between North Korea and the EU begins.

11 September 2001

World Trade Centre in New York attacked.

Autumn–Winter 2001

Approach in the North Korean leadership changed from 'security' to 'economic reform'.

January 2002

George W. Bush designates North Korea as part of the 'axis of evil' in his State of the Union address.

July 2002

New economic policies launched in North Korea.

September 2002

Bush doctrine formulated in the *National Security Strategy of the United States,* published on 17 September 2002. This document is often cited as the definitive statement of the doctrine. It was updated in 2006.

October 2002

Assistant Secretary of State James Kelly visits Pyongyang (negative outcome).

December 2002

IAEA inspectors are asked to leave North Korea.

10 January 2003

North Korea formally withdraws from the Non-Proliferation Treaty.

March 2003
Economic reforms enter a new phase.

16 April 2003
First Commission on Human Rights resolution 2003/10 calls for a 'comprehensive dialogue' with North Korea on human rights.

27–29 August 2003
First round of six-party talks.

2004
Members of the Committee on the Rights of the Child are invited to visit North Korea.

25–28 February 2004
Second round of six-party talks.

15 April 2004
Commission on Human Rights resolution 2004/13. The mandate of Special Rapporteur on North Korea is established by the HR Commission.

28 April 2004
UN Security Council Resolution 1540 on the non-proliferation of weapons of mass destruction.

23–26 June 2004
Third round of six-party talks .

July 2004
Vitit Muntharborn appointed as Special Rapporteur.

18 October 2004
North Korean Human Rights Act passed by US Congress.

10 January 2005
First Special Rapporteur report is followed by the first protest from North Korea.

10 February 2005
North Korea announces that it has become a nuclear power.

14 April 2005
Commission on Human Rights resolution 2005/11 lists widespread human rights violations in North Korea.

19 June–11 August 2006
Human Rights Council first session.

15 July 2006
UN Security Council Resolution 1695 bans the selling of material that would further the ability of North Korea to bolster its ballistic missiles programme.

25 July–7 August 2005
First phase of fourth round of six-party talks.

13–19 September 2005
Second phase of fourth round of six-party talks.

9–11 November 2005
First phase of fifth round of six-party talks.

9 October 2006
First North Korean nuclear test.

14 October 2006
UN Security Council Resolution 1718 imposes sanctions on North Korea.

18–22 December 2006
Second phase of fifth round of six-party talks.

December 2006
North Korea rejects an offer from the office of the High Commissioner of Human Rights of technical cooperation *such as* 'human rights treaty implementation'.

2007–09
The UNDP suspends its activities in North Korea because changes in UNDP practices could not be agreed upon with the North Korean government.

8–13 February 2007
Third phase of fifth round of six-party talks. Agreement on the North Korean nuclear issue.

19–22 March 2007
First phase of sixth round of six-party talks.

18 June 2007
Human Rights Council holds its first meeting.

27–30 September 2007
Second phase of sixth round of six-party talks.

October 2007
Second North–South Korea Summit.

March 2009
Second nuclear test by North Korea.

13 April 2009
UN Presidential Statement announces Security Council intentions to expand sanctions.

14 April 2009
North Korea ends six-party talks. Nuclear inspectors expelled from North Korea. North Korea declares that it will resume its nuclear weapons programme.

25 May 2009
North Korea detonates a nuclear device.

12 June 2009
UN Security Council Resolution 1874. Sanctions tightened.

December 2009–January 2010
North Korea undergoes the Universal Periodic Review.

17 February 2010
Last report of the Special Rapporteur on North Korea, Vitit Muntarbhorn, is published.

March 2010
North Korea Universal Periodic Review adopted by the Human Rights Council.

June 2010
Marzuki Darusman succeeds Muntarbhorn as Special Rapporteur on North Korea.

24 September 2010

The UN Third Committee, in charge of social and humanitarian issues under the auspices of the UN General Assembly, adopts a resolution proposed by the EU and Japan. The resolution condemns North Korea's violation of human rights. It is the sixth resolution of its kind adopted by the committee since 2005, and is submitted to the full UN General Assembly for a vote.

8 April 2011

Human Rights Council resolution. Darusman's mandate extended for one year.

May 2011

Kim Jong-il visits Beijing. A US fact-finding team, led by special envoy on North Korean human rights, Robert King, visits North Korea to look into the food situation.

December 2011

Kim Jong-il dies and is succeeded by his son, Kim Jong-un.

22 March 2012

The Human Rights Council adopts a resolution on North Korea prolonging the mandate of the Special Rapporteur.

22 January 2013

The UN Security Council unanimously approved tighter sanctions on North Korea in retaliation for launching a satellite into space December 12, 2012. This was the third tightening of sanctions since 2006.

12 February 2013

North Korea conducts a third underground nuclear weapons test, prompting further international condemnation and sanctions.

Bibliography

Albright, Madeleine (2003) *Madam Secretary. A Memoir*. Hyperion and New York: Miramax Books.

Alford, C. Fred (1999) *Think No Evil. Korean Values in the Age of Globalization*. Ithaca and London: Cornell University Press.

Baker, Robert (2002) 'Human Rights, Europe and the People's Republic of China', *China Quarterly*, vol. 169, pp. 45–63.

Boerefin, Ineke (2003) 'Human Rights Dialogues', in *Netherlands Quarterly of Human Rights*, vol. 21, no. 1, pp. 3–6.

Chatham House Conference 2010 'Towards a Human Security Framework for North Korea, Promoting Human Rights through Pragmatic Approaches'. December 2–3, 2010.

Chiao, J.Y., Zhang Li, and Tokiki Harada (2008) 'Cultural Neuroscience of Consciousness. From Visual Perceptions to Self-Awareness', in *Journal of Consciousness Studies*, 15, no.10–11, pp. 58–69.

CIA, National Intelligence Estimate (NIE) 42, 14.2-72, no. 288: 'The Two Koreas'.

Cohen, Roberta (1987) 'People's Republic of China: The Human Rights Exception', in *Human Rights Quarterly*, vol. 9, no. 4, pp. 447–549.

Cooper, C.R. and J. Denner (1998) 'Theories linking Culture and Psychology: Universal and Community-Specific Processes', in *Annual Review of Psychology*, vol. 49, pp. 559–584.

The Council of the European Union (2001) 'EU guidelines on human rights dialogues with third countries'.

DIIS Policy Brief (2011) *Dealing with Iran: How Can the EU Achieve Its Strategic Objectives?*

· EU Commission (1995) *Communication of the Commission: A Long-term Policy for China–Europe Relations*. COM (1995) 279/final. See http://eeas.europa.eu/china/docs/com95_279_en.pdf.

FIDH and Human Rights in China (2004) 'Preliminary Assessment of the EU–China Human Rights Dialogue'. Paper submitted to an EU–China HRD meeting: p. 15. On file with the authors.

Fleay, Caroline (2008) 'Engaging in Human rights Diplomacy: The Australia–China Bilateral Dialogue Approach', in *The International Journal of Human Rights*, vol. 12, no. 2, 233–252.

Gosset, David (2002) 'China and Europe: Toward a meaningful relationship'. *Perspectives*, vol. 3, no. 7.

Donald Gregg (2003) *Frontline* interview, 20 February, www.pbs.org/wgbh/pages/frontline/shows/kim/interviews/gregg.html.

Helgesen, Geir (1998) *Democracy and Authority in Korea. The Cultural Dimension in Korean Politics*. London: Curzon Press.

Hecker, Siegfried S. (2006) 'Report on North Korean Nuclear Program'. Center for International Security and Cooperation, Stanford University.

―――― (2010) 'Lessons learned from the North Korean nuclear crises'. *Dædalus*, American Academy of Arts & Sciences.

―――― (2011) 'What I saw in North Korea and why it matters', Google TechTalks at Stanford University, http://www.youtube.com/watch?v=VldRSl7Dc88.

KEDO (1994) 'Agreed Framework between the United States of America and the Democratic People's Republic of Korea' (21 October), www.kedo.org.

Kent, Ann (1999) *China, the United Nations, and Human Rights. The Limits of Compliance*. Philadelphia: University of Pennsylvania Press.

Kinzelbach, Katrin (forthcoming 2013) *The EU's Human Rights Dialogue with China. Quiet Diplomacy and its Limits*. London: Routledge.

Kinzelbach, Katrin and Hatla Thelle (2011) 'Talking Human Rights to China: An Assessment of the EUs Approach', in *The China Quarterly*, no. 205, pp. 60–79.

Korean Central Broadcasting Station (2004) 'US Hostile Policy Disrupting 6-Way Talks', issued 8 October. Compiled and distributed by NTIS, US Dept. of Commerce/World News Connection. Available at www.dialogueselect.com.

Moon, Chung-in (2011) 'The Six party Talks and Implications for a Northeast Asia Nuclear Weapons Free Zone'. Report presented at the East Asia Nuclear Security workshop in Tokyo, 11 November. Available at http://nautilus.org/napsnet.

Mousavian, Seyyed Hossein (2010) *Iran–Europe Relations. Challenges and Opportunities.* London: Routledge, pp. 216–217.

Park, H.S. in C.I. Moon (ed.) (1998) *Understanding Regime Dynamics in North Korea: Contending Perspectives and Comparative Implications.* Seoul: Yonsei University Press.

Park, Han S. (2002) North Korea. *The Politics of Unconventional Wisdom.* Boulder, Colorado: Lynne Rienner

Peerenboom, Randall (2007) *China Modernizes. Threat to the West or Model for the Rest?* Oxford: Oxford University Press.

Perry, William J. and Ashton B. Carter (2002) 'Back to the Brink', in *The Washington Post,* 20 October.

Pinkston, D.A. and P.C. Saunders (2003) 'Seeing North Korea Clearly', in *Survival,* vol. 45, no. 3, pp. 79–102.

Pye, Lucian (1985) *Asian Power and Politics. The Cultural Dimensions of Authority.* Cambridge, Mass. and London: The Belkamp Press of Harvard University Press.

Richter, Thomas and Frauke Seidensticker (2007) 'Evaluation of Switzerland's Human Rights Dialogue with the People's Republic of China'. Deutsches Institut für Menschenrechte, Berlin.

Saccone, Richard (2006) Living with the Enemy: Inside North Korea. Seoul: Hollym International Corp.

Sigal, L.V. (2002) 'North Korea Is No Iraq: Pyongyang's Negotiation Strategy', in Arms Control Today, December.

———— (2003) 'Negotiating with the North' in *Bulletin of the Atomic Scientists,* November–December, vol. 59, no. 6, pp. 19–25.

———— (2006) 'Try engagement for a change', in *Global Asia, The Debate,* Fall, p. 55.

Steinberg, D. (1998) 'Human Rights in North Korea: A Reinter-pretation', in C.I. Moon (ed.), *Understanding Regime Dynamics in North Korea*. Seoul: Yonsei University Press, pp. 241–242.

Tomasevski, Katarina (1997) *Between Sanctions and Elections. Aid Donors and their Human Rights Performance*. London and Washington: Pinter.

Watzlawick, Paul (1976) *How Real is Real? Confusion, Disinformation, Communication*. New York: Vintage Books.

Woodman, Sophia (2004) 'Bilateral Aid to Improve Human Rights: Donors Need to Adopt a More Coherent and Thoughtful Strategy', in *China Perspectives*, no. 51, January–February 2004: p. 29.

Woodman, Sophia and Carole Samdup (2005) 'Canada's Bilateral Human Rights Dialogue with China: Considerations for a Policy Review'. Briefing paper, International Centre for Human Rights and Democratic Development, Montreal, Canada.

Wouters, Jan, a.o. (2007) *EU Human Rights Dialogues. Current Situation, Outstanding Issues and Resources*. Leuven Centre for Global Governance Studies, Policy Brief no. 1.

Index